A Pictorial History: The 1800s-Today

ERIE COUNTY & THE ERIE ISLES

Presented by the Sandusky Register and the Sandusky Library

Acknowledgments

This book would not have been possible without the assistance of the readers of the *Sandusky Register*, who answered the call to help chronicle the history of our community. More than one hundred people provided thousands of photographs, and they also shared their memories of life and of their loved ones. The Sandusky Library's archives librarian, Ron Davidson, and Follett House Museum curator Maggie Marconi also offered their expertise in reviewing and selecting the photos on these pages. The library's board of directors also deserves credit for its support in maintaining a repository of information that tells the bigger story of our community. Finally, credit also goes to *Sandusky Register* staff members William "Bill" Ney, who once again spearheaded this effort, and *Register* librarian Laura Barrett-Bache, who carefully reviewed this book prior to publication.

 • ISBN: 978-1-59725-238-6

Published by Pediment Publishing, a division of The Pediment Group, Inc. www.pediment.com Printed in Canada.

Table of Contents

Foreword

The concept of photography goes back centuries, and in some ways can be linked to the ancient drawings of hieroglyphics on the walls of the caves where man first lived. But the first true photographic image was achieved in 1814, and that set the stage for this book of photographs.

During most of the 19th century, while the art of photography was being invented, it was the province of men of science who tested, re-tested, refined and developed the methods that allowed the capture of images. By the end of the century, it was fast becoming open to families through a rapidly developing technology.

From the age of Kodak and instamatics to digital photography, this book chronicles life here in the Heartland from very near to the beginning of the great American experiment. It was made possible by those early inventors and by the readers of the *Register*, who provided most of the photographs on these pages.

Matt Westerhold
Managing editor
Sandusky Register

THE 1800S

Born of the American Revolution, the Firelands was settled in the early 1800s and evolved, much as the rest of the nation, into a powerhouse of pioneers, entrepreneurs and men and women of strength and courage. We were a community and a nation made up of the sons and daughters of revolutionaries and new immigrants, who all believed in the great American experiment.

We thrived in it.

From our heritage rooted in an agrarian economy through years of formation and reformation, we grew as a community, as a state and a nation. Wounded and slowed by a cholera epidemic, and the great Civil War that divided the nation, we survived and thrived during the 19th century despite the conflicts, despite the challenge.

And like the rest of the planet, we discovered together the world of photography and began chronicling our lives in black and white.

Sloane House hotel on the corner of Columbus Avenue and Washington Row, circa 1900. *Courtesy of Sue LaFene*

Sandusky High School class of 1872. The teachers include: Ms. Welingson, Mrs. Hoffman and Mrs. S. Amslie. The class includes: Ella Rayl, Alex Camp, Emma Alder, Hattie Kuch, Henry Moore, Laura Wetherell, Alice Kinney, Ella Kelham, Hattie Miller, Frank Barker, Emma Hager, Robert Walsh, Emmile Williams, Lula Hayer, Charles McLauth and Antonio Springer.

Courtesy of Sandusky Library

John Kastor I at Camp Cleveland in Geauga County Fairgrounds, Aug. 27, 1862. He enlisted as a member of the Sandusky Jagercompagnie, a group of German-born patriots that was reorganized as Company F of the 107th Volunteer Regiment of the Ohio Infantry under Captain Louis Traub. He was discharged to Charleston, South Carolina, July 10, 1865.

Courtesy of Linda Kastor Layton

Henry Ritter with wife, circa 1875. He operated a cigar business on Columbus Avenue from the 1860s until his death. The business was best known for the wooden statue "Punch" that stood at the front of the store for over 60 years.

Courtesy of Mrs. William (Lata Hitchcock) Ritter

Tritschler & Smith Meat Market at West Market Street, circa 1875.

Courtesy of John L. Crooks

Downtown Sandusky in the 1880s. *Courtesy of Robert and Karen Deitz*

Celebration sponsored by the Active Turnverein, a German social and athletic club also known as the "Turners," on Water Street, July 5, 1886.

Courtesy of Roger L. Dickman

Erie County Courthouse was built in 1874. *Courtesy of Robert and Karen Deitz*

Hartley family from Berlin Township, circa 1890, left to right: J. W., Thomas, Kyle and Ellen. *Courtesy of Tom Hartley*

Bahnsen contractor wagon at Meigs and Monroe streets, circa 1890. Men on the wagon, left to right: J. P. Bahnsen, Jim Rumford, Sidney Bahnsen and James Rumford. The Bahnsens also bought horses to sell to local farmers.
Courtesy of Jim and Brenda Bahnsen

Confirmation of Minnie Heckelman from St. John's Evangelical Church on Thomas Road in Monroeville, circa 1890. *Courtesy of Julie Mingus Koegle*

Erie County Infirmary on Columbus Avenue, circa 1890. *Courtesy of Sue LaFene*

Louis and Katherine Herbel Ebert and their 14 children, Erie County, circa 1895. In front is Anna Maude with twins Gustave and Hilda. Seated in the middle row: Elizabeth, Margaretta, Louis Sr. holding George, Minnie, Luella, Katherine and Louis Jr. Standing in back: John, Emma, Jacob, Charles and Katherine. They held annual family reunions starting in 1936 and into the 1960s. The reunions for many years were held at Oxford Grange Hall on Taylor and Mason roads that later became a private residence. Their descendants resumed the tradition in August 2008.

Courtesy of Cherie James

Leonard Charles Catri in Huron, 1897. He was the father of Alton Catri, Nick Catri and Anthony Catri.
Courtesy of Joseph L. Catri

Erie County Courthouse on Columbus Avenue in the late 1800s.
Courtesy of Sue LaFene

Funeral of Samuel Edison in Milan, February 1896. Left to right: unidentified behind fence, Mr. Stoddard, unidentified behind tree, Nancy Wadsworth, Elizabeth Root Willcox, Marion Edison Page, Thomas Edison and Homer Page. *Courtesy of Marla Higgins*

Kuebeler Brewery on Tiffin Avenue, circa 1895. *Courtesy of Sue LaFene*

THE EARLY 1900S

By the turn of the 20th century, there was just 10 miles of paved road across the span of the nation. But the automobile industry was being born, and it would come to dominate the century economically, across the nation and here, in the heart of the Heartland.

By 1908, Henry Ford built his first Model T and began redefining the nature of work, of jobs and of society.

Across the Firelands we built schools and churches that stand to this day and continue to serve the community, including the Sandusky Library. We formed clubs and service agencies that also continue a mission, and we shared a love for our lives in our community.

And we snapped photos of our lives that would, in the end, tell us the story of our community.

Crew of the steamer *R. B. Hayes* that ran from Sandusky to Cedar Point, circa 1900. *Courtesy of Robert and Karen Deitz*

Edward Brengartner in front of his store at 746 E. Water St., circa 1900.
Courtesy of Randy Catri

Quinne Bay Club fishing party at North Bass Island, circa 1900. George Axtell is on the far left in the front row. *Courtesy of Dale A. Hartlaub*

Tritschler Meat Market at Camp and Washington streets, circa 1900. Left to right: Andrew Tritschler Sr., unidentified and Lawrence Tritschler.
Courtesy of John L. Crooks

Sloane Block with Sloane House hotel on Washington Row and Columbus Avenue, 1900. *Courtesy of Sue LaFene*

Workers at the Richards Hotel, Lakeside, circa 1900. Emily Petersen is in the center of the back row. *Courtesy of Marie Severance*

West Huron baseball team, circa 1900. Front row, left to right: William Lundy, Myron Osborne and Martin Purcell. Middle row: William Hinde, Tom Lundy, Ed Everett and George Hinde. Back row: James Dildine, Sam Purcell, Charley Dildine, Ed Hughes and Frank Everett. *Courtesy of Donald G. Everett*

Lentz family, circa 1902, left to right: Clara, Elizabeth, Jacob, Jacob Sr., Mary, Liz and Edwin. Jacob Sr., a German immigrant, was a part of the chain migration of the 1850s when one family would sponsor another family to come to America. The Marshall family sponsored him and he then married their daughter, Elizabeth. A stonemason, he came to Sandusky because of the limestone. *Courtesy of Pamela Moyer and Marsha Bennett Scott*

Sandusky coal and ore docks, circa 1905. On the right is the original number one dumper and on the left side the cars are being unloaded with clam shell cranes. These cranes were eventually replaced with the number two coal dumper. *Courtesy of George Mingus*

Sandusky's Stars baseball team, circa 1900. Front row, left to right: Bob Koegle, Fred Kubach, Frank "Spot" McConnville and unidentified. Second row: Frank "Happy" Hegner, Joe Hegner, unidentified and unidentified. Third row: Eddie Hemmerle, Charlie Murphy, Charlie "Pink" Bogert, George Upp and Jim Talbot. Fourth row: unidentified, manager Ed Geason, unidentified and (unknown) Murschel. *Courtesy of Julie Koegle*

The Standard Oil Co. bulk station trucks and drivers at Campbell Street, 1905. Third person from the left is Russell Bertsch. *Courtesy of James A. and Martha Bertsch*

Mrs. Hummel's home, circa 1900. Francis Fiegelist is in the black dress.
Courtesy of Donna Greene

Mary Scherer with mother Mrs. Mary Scherer standing in front of their home at McKelvey Street, 1900. The house was next door to the Sandusky Paint Co. It burned down in 2002. *Courtesy of Merita Wright*

U.S. Coast Guard station at Marblehead, circa 1900. The original station was built in 1876. *Courtesy of Marie Severance*

Kelleys Island Winery around the turn of the century. The winery was destroyed by fire in 1934. *Courtesy of Charles "Jake" Martin*

St. Stephen German Evangelical Church erected in 1882 at Jefferson and Poplar streets, 1905. *Courtesy of Janis Burke*

At Ohly's Drugstore on the corner of East Adams Street and Columbus Avenue, circa 1908. Left to right: Lena, Lewis, Stuart and Nelson Ohly.
Courtesy of Brenda Bahnsen compliments of Ruth Baker

Cutting ice in Sandusky Bay, 1908. *Courtesy of Mrs. Lester Syrstad*

Sailboat on Sandusky Bay, 1908. *Courtesy of Mrs. Lester Syrstad*

At Blue Hole in Castalia, Sept. 1, 1908, left to right: Ted Koegle, Edith Biehl and Esther Biehl. *Courtesy of Martha Barnhart*

Geo. M. Rinkleff Hardware on West Water Street, 1909. *Courtesy of Mrs. Lester Syrstad*

St. Mary's School on Decatur Street, 1909. *Courtesy of Sue LaFene*

At Richardson Restaurant in Port Clinton, July 24, 1908. Andrew Westerhold is on the left. *Courtesy of Jim Westerhold*

1910–1919

A labor movement and an urbanization of America were part of the community's fabric by 1910. By the latter years of the decade we joined our nation's war to end all wars. We believed it was possible because we still believed in the great American experiment.

By the beginning of the century, more than 3.6 million immigrants had come to the United States, and many of them settled here, where neighborhoods and religious and social organizations formed along the lines of our ethnic backgrounds.

We built lives around our families, our schools and churches, our clubs and affiliations, our community.

The moving picture shows were fast becoming a dominant American pastime, and we enjoyed our sport and recreation in America's Vacationland.

Relatives in Sandusky, circa 1912, left to right: Helen and Henry Papke, Marie Papke, Theresa Harder, Carl Papke, Alma Erdman and Anna and Max Papke. *Courtesy of Renee Barrett*

Chippewa and *Lakeside III* docked at Kelleys Island, 1910. *Courtesy of Charles "Jake" Martin*

Long Point on Kelleys Island. *Courtesy of Charles "Jake" Martin*

Interior of the Mertz Store on Washington Street, circa 1910. *Courtesy of Robert and Karen Deitz*

Herman and Mary Crecelius farm on Bryan Road in Milan, 1910. Albert Crecelius is on the pony. Herman Crecelius is with the buggy and team of horses. Mary Crecelius is with the horse and colt. Edith Hart, the house lady, is in the buggy in front of the barn door, and William Schug, farm hand, is in the wagon. In the buggy in front on the right are Paul and Arvata Crecelius. *Courtesy of James Crecelius*

Standing in the back of a boat he built is William Shepherd, postmaster, circa 1910. The Berlin Street Bridge over the Huron River is in the background. *Courtesy of Randy Catri*

One of the earliest airplanes in the area landing at Cedar Point Beach, 1910. *Courtesy of Mrs. Lester Syrstad*

Line of cars on Washington Row, circa 1910. *Courtesy of Robert and Karen Deitz*

St. Stephen German Evangelical Church at Jefferson and Poplar streets, 1910. Front row, left to right: Stuart Ohly, Esther Ramm, (unknown) Ramm, unidentified, unidentified, unidentified, Hulda Egli and Roy Klueglein. Second row: Mrs. Kohloff, Mrs. Hasseberg, Mrs. Schiller, Mrs. Bahrle, Pastor Egli, Mrs. Egli, Mrs. Bremer, unidentified, Mrs. Bergman, Mrs. Wendschuh and Mrs. Windisch. Third row: Mrs. Lenz, Mrs. Stoffel, unidentified, Mrs. Ross, Mrs. Meinzer, unidentified, Mrs. Ohle, Mr. Bahnsen, unidentified, Mrs. Zimmerman, Mrs. Wassner, Miss Katie Ohly, unidentified, unidentified, Mrs. Bohn, unidentified, Mrs. Ohly, unidentified, Mrs. Klueglein and unidentified. Back row: Mrs. Uhl, Mrs. Mayer, Mame Beahrle, Clara Zimmerman Rossiter, Mrs. Gaa, unidentified, Mrs. Lewis Ohle, Mrs. Windisch, Mrs. Hemsen, Mrs. George Schiller, Mrs. Bahnsen, unidentified and Mrs. Thierry. The girls on the porch are Cora Beahrle and Mable Bock. *Courtesy of Janis Burke*

Sophia Winterhalter Westerhold at Put-in-Bay, June 26, 1910. *Courtesy of Jim Westerhold*

Donahue Hardware Co. and Stubig Shoe store on West Water Street, 1910. *Courtesy of Mrs. Lester Syrstad*

At Cedar Point Beach, circa 1910. *Courtesy of Donna Greene*

Fishing fleet cutting through icy water at the foot of Columbus Avenue, 1910. *Courtesy of Mrs. Lester Syrstad*

Confirmation class of St. John's United Church of Christ at 2712 Mason Rd. in Oxford Township in Milan, April 16, 1911. Front row, left to right: Anna Ries, Elizabeth Bauers, Elsie Loos, Esther Crecelius and Katherine Mowry. Second row: Homer Crecelius, Melvin Mowry, Hulda Leber, Anna Kellog, Alma Schaefer, Mabel Ohlemacher, Amanda Schaefer, George Thorn and Fred Ries. Third row: Jennie Asmus, Freida Wallrabenstein, Clara Hoffman, Eva Weilnau, Luella Gutzeit, Edith Weilnau, Stella Leber and Walter Rebel. Fourth row: Carl Weilnau, Harry Rebel, Fred Gastier, Lyn Kellog and Walter Scheid. Back row: Emil Ries, Amelia Sengstalk, Carri Gutzeit, Bob Bowers and Fred Heckelman. In the far back is Rev. Gustav B. Kreuzenstein. *Courtesy of Joyce Schaefer*

Fish catch at the Sandusky waterfront on Water Street, circa 1913.

Courtesy of Sue LaFene

In front of the John G. Gunzenhauser Meat Market in Huron, 1914.

Courtesy of Roger L. Dickman

Young Men's Society Juniors basketball team champions, 1911–13, left to right: Ralph Schafer, Cyril Daniel, Ralph Smith, Rolf Michael, Arthur Schropp and Paul Westerhold. *Courtesy of Jim Westerhold*

Five cousins at Cedar Point, 1914, left to right: Marion Eck, Millie Bookerman, Adeline Platte, Clarice Platte and Walter F. Platte. *Courtesy of Walter Platte*

Boat docks at Put-in-Bay, July 1914. *Courtesy of Barbara Ott*

Filling a silo at Meadow Brook farm in Berlin Township, 1915.
Courtesy of John Hartman and Ethel Smith

Parker Mill, circa 1915. It was operated by John H. Parker from 1913 to 1919. On March 29, 1919, it became the Castalia Elevator, a co-operative grain handler for area farmers. *Courtesy of Bruce Martin*

Performing men's quartet, circa 1916. Included: unidentified, Charles Abbey, Will Trost, Clarence Foster and Charles Buck. *Courtesy of Jackie Mayer*

Lakeside Pavilion, circa 1915. *Courtesy of Marie Severance*

Roy Smith and an unidentified friend on the newly-paved Cedar Point Road, 1913. *Courtesy of Edward Boose*

Central Dock on North Bass Island, October 1914. Evert Fox is with the horse and buggy. William Axtell is bailing water in the boat *Bouncer* in the foreground. Herman Dussau is standing on the dock over a boat. Peg Dibert is seated next to Herman. Beatrice Axtell's back is to the camera, seated on the wagon. The old Kenny Hall and Lay Brothers twin house is on shore. *Courtesy of Dale A. Hartlaub*

Silvan and Marcella Ehrnsberger at Cedar Point Beach, circa 1915. *Courtesy of Sherri Dominick*

Sandusky Council #275 United Commercial Travelers in front of the Erie County Courthouse, June 12, 1915. *Courtesy of Sue LaFene*

On Cedar Point Beach, August 1915, left to right: Irene Delbo, Lester Curtis and Irene Greenfelder. *Courtesy of Edward Boose*

Sts. Peter and Paul School, 1916. Ruth Everett is on the upper left. *Courtesy of Tom and MaryLou Gundlach*

Employees of Sandusky Glass Co., Sunday, May 28, 1916. *Courtesy of Robert and Karen Deitz*

Albert Royer with a cask at A. Schmidt Jr. and Sons winery, Jan. 17, 1918. *Courtesy of Elizabeth Riems*

Sandusky High School football team, 1918. Albert William Crecelius is in the middle row on the left. *Courtesy of John and Alvina Schaeffer*

Part of Team #40 War League Workers at Berlin Heights Town Hall, circa 1917. Front row, left to right: Rev. William Cady, S. L. Hill, F. S. Fowler, Fred Ackerman and Charles Hoffman. Back row: William Moats, L. C. Meyers, J. K. Boehm and George Hartman. *Courtesy of John Hartman and Ethel Smith*

Gasoline delivery truck driven by Russell Bertsch at Campbell Street at the railroad tracks, circa 1918. *Courtesy of James A. and Martha Bertsch*

Scherer family at their home on Remington Avenue, 1918. Front row, left to right: Mrs. Mary Scherer, John Scherer and Ruth Steinhauser. Back row: Mr. and Mrs. Henry Scherer, Dorothy Scherer, Mrs. Minnie Scherer and Mrs. Mary Steinhauser. *Courtesy of Merita Wright*

Louis and Eleanor Meyers at their family farm in Berlin Heights, July 4, 1918. *Courtesy of Dick Koegle*

Irene Humes Toft at the Ohio Veterans Home, 1919. *Courtesy of Gary R. Mussell*

"Re-making of a Nation" showing at the Schade Theatre, circa 1918. *Courtesy of Robert and Karen Deitz*

The 1920s

The nation accepted its mothers, sisters and daughters, granting women the full sense of citizenship with the passage of the 19th Amendment to the U.S. Constitution and the right to vote in 1920.

The battles had just begun, however, as national legislators outlawed the "sin juice" and Prohibition, and all it entailed, dominated the decade.

The great American experiment continued, and families across the region would soon be faced with what all the nation would grapple with — a great economic depression that would carry us through the end of the decade and on through all of the next.

But through it all, we documented the triumphs and the tragedies, the awesome powers of nature and the simple, rewarding moments of family, of community.

Home of Anna Hall on East Market Street after a tornado, June 28, 1924. *Courtesy of Donna Greene*

At Hornbach's Cooper Shop, circa 1920, left to right: the boss, William Eschenauer and a co-worker. *Courtesy of Donna Green*

Huron High School students on the steps of the school, 1920. *Courtesy of Tom Hartley*

Family gathering at the Biehl home at 1007 Hancock St., circa 1920. In the front row, left to right: Jena Biehl Schrank; George Kneisel; his sister, Anna Kneisel Biehl; and her husband, Henry Jacob Biehl. *Courtesy of Martha Barnhart*

H. L. Peeke, known as "Judgie," at his home on Columbus Avenue and Gilcher Court, circa 1920. He was an attorney and judge, and he ran for U.S. President on the Prohibition Party ticket. *Courtesy of Jackie Mayer*

Corner of Division Street and Lake Shore on Kelleys Island, circa 1920. *Courtesy of Charles "Jake" Martin*

Mail boat making its way across frozen Lake Erie on its way to Kelleys Island, circa 1920. *Courtesy of Charles "Jake" Martin*

Limestone crusher on the south side of Kelleys Island. The light plant on the far right, owned by Fred Martin, supplied the electricity to the quarry. The train would come on the tracks on top and dump its load into the crusher. *Courtesy of Charles "Jake" Martin*

The steamer *Chippewa* coming into the downtown dock at Kelleys Island. The dock was owned by the Kelleys Island Steamboat Company, circa 1920. *Courtesy of Charles "Jake" Martin*

In front of the Glass Works on Milan Road, circa 1920. *Courtesy of Marie Severance*

Swimmers in Sandusky Bay, circa 1920. *Courtesy of Robert and Karen Deitz*

Prominent Sandusky businessmen and the pastor at St. Mary's Church, circa 1920. Front row, left to right: unidentified, Andrew Westerhold, Msgr. Fashnacht and Louis Andres. Back row: Norbert Erney, Frank Ritzenthaler, Ralph Smith, Anson Singler and John Scales. *Courtesy of Jim Westerhold*

Guests being served a meal on the porch of the Mansion, which provided rooms for tourists in Sandusky, circa 1920. Standing in the back is Hannah Earle, proprietor of the Mansion. *Courtesy of Tom and MaryLou Gundlach*

Ohio Public Service Co. streetcar, circa 1920, that ran from Marblehead to Toledo through Oak Harbor. Louis Bennett was the superintendent. He later served as distribution superintendent of Ohio Public Service Co. in the Port Clinton Division and then was transferred to Sandusky.
Courtesy of Robert and Karen Deitz

Charles Westerhold, left, with sister Virginia in a stroller sled, Jan. 21, 1922.
Courtesy of Jim Westerhold

Andrew Westerhold's family car, a Studebaker, Aug. 20, 1922. Included are Charles, Sophia, Virginia and Olga Westerhold. *Courtesy of Jim Westerhold*

Albert F. Keech by the B. F. Keech Groceries delivery wagon, 1924. Albert inherited the business from his parents, Albert and Christina, who started the store. In 1924 Albert married Viola B. Pankow, 17 years younger, and the couple had ten children, with two sets of twins. *Courtesy of Robert U. Keech*

Huron School fourth graders, 1921. Carl Wechter is in the second row, fourth from the left; Rockie Larizza, third row, fifth from the left; Tom Hartley, third row, sixth from the left; Naomi Deyo, fourth row, far left; and Helen Hoffman, fourth row, seventh from the left. *Courtesy of Aileen Hartley*

Table rock at Long Point on Kelleys Island. The rock was tumbled over by a high wind storm in the 1930s. *Courtesy of Charles "Jake" Martin*

Inside Johns' Dry Goods Store at 331 Camp St., circa 1925. It was owned by John and Carrie Tritschler Johns. *Courtesy of John L. Crooks*

Virginia Schmidt Grathwol pushing the pram with one-year-old Rose Elizabeth Heyman on Central Avenue, 1924. *Courtesy of Janis Burke*

Tornado damage in Sandusky, June 1924. *Courtesy of Dale A. Hartlaub*

Cranes pulling a train engine out of the bay at the entrance to the cove on the city's east side following the tornado of June 1924. *Courtesy of Sandusky Library*

Kilbourne Cooperage following the tornado of June 1924. *Courtesy of Sandusky Library*

Frank E. Delius Sr. with his Model T Ford on the family farm on Fox Road one-quarter mile west of Milan Road, circa 1922.
Courtesy of Robert Delius

Physicians, board members and clergy of Providence Hospital, May 4, 1924. *Courtesy of Dale A. Hartlaub*

Edward Brengarther, sales agent, selling lots for the Old Homestead-on-the-Lake at Cleveland Road in Huron, 1927. *Courtesy of Randy Catri*

Juanita Toft at 1413 W. Taylor St., 1925. *Courtesy of Gary R. Mussell*

Children born at Providence Hospital on Hospital Day, May 12, 1924. *Courtesy of Dale A. Hartlaub*

Third-grade class at St. Mary's School, 1926–27. Front row, left to right: Genevieve Moos, Alvin Kaman, Mary Michel, Mary Kramer, Alvin Beihl and (unknown) Mahling. Second row: Vera Kanzler, Marjorie Felter, Ellen Elsner, (unknown) Gundlach, Ruth Renwand and Gretchen Bing. Back row: unidentified, Helen Curtis, Mary Beilstien, unidentified and (unknown) Hemerick. *Courtesy of Lynn Montelauro*

The Toft family at Camp and West Taylor streets, circa 1926. On the far left are Mike and Irene Toft with their two daughters, Eileen and Juanita. *Courtesy of Gary R. Mussell*

Ruth Bristol Ohly and Nelson Ohly at the beach, circa 1925. Nelson was a pharmacist at Ohly's Drugstore at Columbus Avenue and East Adams Street. *Courtesy of Ruth Baker*

Virginia Schmidt Grathwol with child Rose Heyman near stacked cannon balls at Put-in-Bay Waterfront Park, July 1925. *Courtesy of Janis Burke*

Employees of the Lake Shore Electric Railway on the roof of a downtown Sandusky building, circa 1925. From left to right: Ray Walter, Charles Evans, Ralph Sayles, A. F. Maxwell, Stanley Davis, J. Letterman and Lawrence Witter. *Courtesy of Ford Evans*

Harriet Marie Leslie at age seven, 1927. She grew up at 511 Gartland Ave. in Sandusky. *Courtesy of Cherie James*

Msgr. William Zierolf with the first communion class at St. Mary's Church, May 22, 1927. *Courtesy of Judy Hippler*

Playing at Cedar Point Beach, circa 1927. Left to right: Tony Elsholz, Clara Elsholz, Catherine Federkiel, Doris Lentz and Doloris Lentz.
Courtesy of Marsha Bennett Scott

Picnic at Catawba Island, September 1928. Included are Vera Curtis, Elsa Sonntag, Mrs. Zistel, Billy Allendorf, Ruth Allendorf, Alice Sonntag, Jean Curtis, August Allendorf, Auda Aires, Miriam Curtis, Norma Zistel, Earl Curtis and Day Aires. *Courtesy of Miriam Porto*

G. A. Boeckling traveling from Columbus Avenue to Cedar Point Amusement Park, circa 1928. *Courtesy of Nancy Grathwol*

THE 1930S

Our fathers, our mothers, our grandmothers and our grandfathers survived the worst economic times in our nation's history, and came out the other end to confront a world at war, again.

We took any jobs and built parks and other projects through government work programs, determined to survive the worst of times.

Our downtowns were the centers of community commerce, and our churches and civic organizations helped get us through the hard times.

An advertisement photo for selling Wonder Bread at Gundlach Grocery at 2231 Columbus Avenue, 1939, left to right: Leo Gundlach, Ruth Gundlach, Tommy Gundlach and Bud Angus. *Courtesy of Tom and MaryLou Gundlach*

Interior of Spalla Grocery at 1106 W. Washington St., circa 1930. Left to right: Charles, five years old; Joseph, seven years old; and their father Antonino "Tony" Spalla. The family lived behind the store. *Courtesy of Anthony J. Spalla*

Curtis family at New York Central Depot on Depot Street, circa 1930, left to right: Ada and Howe Willis, Vera and Earl Curtis, Lynn Curtis, Vera Jean Curtis and Miriam Curtis. *Courtesy of Miriam Porto*

Trap shooting at the Kelley Mansion, circa 1930. *Courtesy of Charles "Jake" Martin*

Gathering wildflowers in Berlin Heights, 1930, left to right: Martha Sontag, Miriam Curtis, Alice Sontag, Vera Curtis and Jean Curtis.
Courtesy of Miriam Porto

Sister Mary Isidore in the laboratory of Providence Hospital, April 7, 1931.
Courtesy of Dale A. Hartlaub

Strickfaden service station on Columbus Avenue and Taylor Road in Perkins Township, circa 1937. The owner was Joseph C. Strickfaden, and the business was a gas station, auto repair, general store and ice cream parlor.
Courtesy of Dona Ehrhardt

MaryLou Ritter with cousin William Ritter at Grandmother Ritter's summer cottage at Cedar Point Chaussee, 1932. *Courtesy of Mrs. William (Lata Hitchcock) Ritter*

Ice skating in Sandusky Bay, 1932. Left to right: Karl Rinderle, Mary Lee Graefe and Oliver Rinderle. *Courtesy of Miriam Porto*

Osborne School, circa 1938. Jody Gast is the fifth child from the left in the back row. *Courtesy of Brenda Bahnsen*

Posing for a photo at Cedar Point, 1932, left to right: Laura Miles, Lois House Parker, Elsa Dwight and Kathryn Tritschler Crooks. *Courtesy of John L. Crooks*

Confirmation class of St. Paul's Lutheran Church, April 9, 1933. Juanita Toft is in the front row on the far right. *Courtesy of Gary R. Mussell*

William Everett reading the news on his front porch at Milan Road, 1931.
Courtesy of Tom and MaryLou Gundlach

Huron High School reserve basketball champs, 1939. Front row, left to right: Ted Hahn, Joe Wallace, Jack Ranft, Ralph Pisano and Wayne Klein. Back row: Ira Bailey, Duane Rawft, Frank Ritter and coach T. W. Hartley. *Courtesy of Aileen Hartley*

Getting ready for a neighborhood parade in the backyard of the Daniel home, 1934. Standing: Bill Daniel, Paul Swank and Earl McGreavey. On the tricycle are Bob and John Daniel with Mary Daniel to their right. Others are unidentified. *Courtesy of Bob Daniel*

175-pound sturgeon caught in a gill net at Kelleys Island, circa 1935. From left to right: Alfred McKillips, Bert Kugler and Sylvester Dwelle, all from Kelleys Island. The fish had 60 pounds of eggs, which were selling at $1.00 per pound. The fish and eggs together brought well over $100. This is the largest ever caught at Kelley's Island; one caught at Pelee Island more recently weighed 190 pounds. *Courtesy of Wilbur F. Ramsey*

Works Progress Administration office and investigative personnel, 1936. Clarence Crooks is in the back row, second from the right. Elizabeth Tritschler is in the front row, third from the left. *Courtesy of John L. Crooks*

Confirmation class at St. Stephen Evangelical Church, 1938. Included: Marilyn M. Bitter, Leroy M. Borman, Robert O. Burre, Lois J. Gassan, Rolland B. Hartenfeld, Idamae J. Huntley, Donald L. Leech, Bette D. Mowry, Mary J. Panzer, Paul H. Pheiffer, Harry C. Robinson, Jeanette A. Russell, John R. Sprau, Harold G. Spinello, Malcolm G. Seitz, Eugene E. Stookey, Marion F. Thomas, Alta M. Watzel, Garwood G. Fenton, Catherine M. Fisher and Thomas G. Neill. Rev. Dr. H. E. Pheiffer is in the front row, center. *Courtesy of Janis Burke*

Trap shooting club called the Okoboji Indians, June 16, 1936. The club was based at Cedar Point.

Courtesy of Peter A. Wennes

Secondo Williams and his accordian band entertained groups throughout the Sandusky area, circa 1938. Williams is fourth from the left.

Courtesy of Elizabeth Riems

Wedding of Cletis Weyer and Ruth Mesenburg, Aug. 8, 1939. Left to right: Ruth, Cletis, Margaret Keller, George Mitler, Agnes Tommas, Melvin Riedy, Dorothy Mesenburg and Walter Mesenburg. *Courtesy of Judy Hippler*

Drum and Bugle Corps sponsored by the Veterans of Foreign Wars, October 1939. Front row: Mr. Wedeman, Wayne White, Jack Woodruff, Audrey Butts, Betty Simon, Kathryn Wagner, Joyce Schneider, Cecelia Sartor, Rosemary Subcasky, Marilyn Smith, Mary Ann Lockey, Katherine Herzog, Billy Busam, Junior Bickley, Tommy Scavio, Junior Sartor, Cyril Riedy and Mr. Pfanner. Back row: Mr. Woodruff, Mike Dienes, Paul Schwank, Vincent Kaufman, Beverly Binsack, Mildred Hamburger, Jean Pfanner, Dorothy Seil, Dorothy Zeck, Maxine Scott, Betty Royer, June Kaufman, Paul Royer, Bob Pfanner, Dick Stark, Johnie Behrendsen, Harold Bauer and Mr. Ziegler. *Courtesy of Elizabeth Riems*

Confirmation class of Zion Lutheran Church, 1938. Margaret Sehlmeyer is included. *Courtesy of Gary R. Mussell*

Six-year-old concert pianist Rosemary Schultz before her concert on the Steinway Concert Grand piano at Sandusky High School auditorium, circa 1938. She is with the ushers for the program, left to right: Pauline Schultz, Virginia Caswell, Audrey Schultz, Jeanne Pfanner, Millie Bores and Charlotte Baier. *Courtesy of Rosemary S. Schultz Pove*

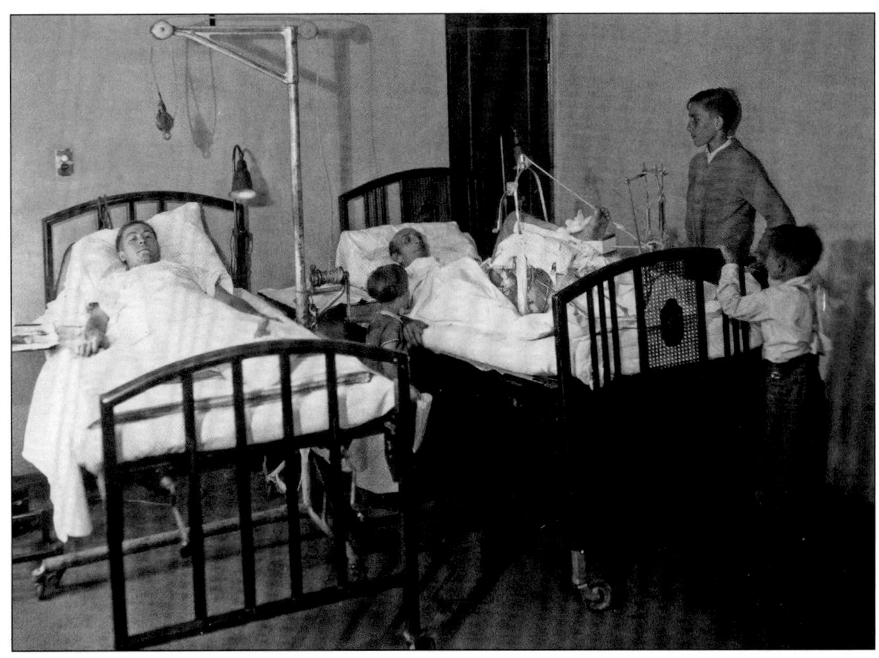

Men's ward at Providence Hospital, Sept. 3, 1938. *Courtesy of Dale A. Hartlaub*

Members of the Rye Beach Roller Club of Huron at the Huron Park, Nov. 18, 1939. The roller skating group is on their way to a production at the Detroit Arena Gardens. *Courtesy of Edward Boose*

Sandusky High School graduates Edith and Merlin Lamb at Hancock Street, 1937. *Courtesy of Anthony Schaefer*

THE 1940S

We planted our Victory Gardens with other Americans across the country, and we believed President Franklin D. Roosevelt when he told us "the only thing we have to fear was fear itself."

Men and women here joined forces to defeat the Nazis in World War II, and women joined the work force in record numbers to take jobs that men left behind when they went to war.

We bought and sold war bonds, used our gas rationing tickets judiciously and had scrap metal drives to support the war effort. We fought for our country, both here and abroad.

We mourned our war dead but never lost our resolve.

We supported the war effort here at home and embraced our returning heroes, who came home to a new, faster-paced lifestyle that marked the beginning of an era we who are alive today would come to know.

Apex Manufacturing during World War II. Marie Leslie Byington is in the back wearing a white shirt with an apron. *Courtesy of Cherie James*

Esmond Dairy on Campbell Street, circa 1940, left to right: Rudolph Guerich, George Balduff, Basil Glass, Frank Tepley, Fred Mainzer, Del DeLor and Clyde Gentry. *Courtesy of Virginia Bohn*

Huron High School class of 1940 play cast. Included are Bob Taylor, Emma Makvich, Virginia Kreilic, Horace Mitchell, Joann Taylor, Magaline Temper, John Bartzen, Tom Hammond, Wayne Klein, Jack Ranft, Irene Cassidy, Irene Vanci, Gladys Goodsite and Clara Dircks. *Courtesy of Sue Frankart*

Eleanor Koegle by the cash register at Tea Co. Inn at Ohio 113 and 61 in Berlin Heights, circa 1940. She and her husband, Dick, took over the business from her parents, Roy and Minnie Meyers.

Courtesy of Julie Mingus Koegle

At their mother's house on Venice Road, circa 1940, left to right: Roland Ziemke, Idella Ziemke Hitchcock, Lila Ziemke, Arline Ziemke Hine, Ina Ziemke Whetstone and Loretta Ziemke Horton.

Courtesy of Mrs. William (Lata Hitchcock) Ritter

Osborne School yard, 1940. Front row, left to right: Bob Hill, Russel Meisler, unidentified, Jim Roberts, Jim Mann, unidentified, Herbert Hoelzer, unidentified, Paul Hoelzer and J. Sprat. Second row: Donna Loffer, Mary Ann Westcott, unidentified, Penelope Tighe, Marilyn Gast, unidentified, Gloria Doyle, Claudine Kessler, Helen Richter, Lynnette Geiser and Margaret Hoyer. Third row: Luvada Stovall, Helen Johnson, Marilyn Kalk, unidentified, Bob Betz, teacher M. Cole, unidentified, unidentified, Jim Robinson, Jean Shepherd, Lois Alton and Audrey Babcock.

Courtesy of Lynnette M. Galloway

Lawrence Smith residence on Harris Road, circa 1940. Left to right: Lawrence, Lyle, Paul and Alma Schaefer Smith. Kneeling in the front is Billie Smith with Pooch.

Courtesy of Brenda Bahnsen compliments of Ruth Baker

William Parks Harris, circa 1940. He served Erie County as Chief Deputy Auditor for 38 years. He died on his last day of work.

Courtesy of Robert and Karen Deitz

Rev. Mason and Rev. Hester burning the mortgage at Second Baptist Church, circa 1945. Built in 1849, the congregation of the church was active in the Underground Railroad during the Civil War. *Courtesy of Joan D. Cooper*

Past presidents of the VFW auxiliary, circa 1940. Front row, left to right: Angelline Corso, Bess Watters, Leona Gentry, Ruby Stone and Nell Biglin. Back row: Metta Braun, Edna Oswald, Marion Glass, Marguerite Sheets and Clara Moore. *Courtesy of Virginia Bohn*

Emily Petersen working on the press at Philco producing radio parts, circa 1940. *Courtesy of Marie Severance*

Cletis Weyer riding his scooter on Skadden Road in Margaretta Township, July 1942. *Courtesy of Judy Hippler*

Miss Keller's second-grade class at Perkins School, 1942–43. Front row, left to right: Marilyn Spencer, Judy Gerold, Lynette Held, Francis Robertson, Lenore LaBuy, Marilyn Potts, Margaret Green and unidentified. Second row: unidentified, Jack Best, unidentified, Marlene Toft, Maryann Beatty, Pat Moore, John Bintz, Jim Dee, unidentified and unidentified. Back row: Ron Dee, Jack Klien, Robert Schwanger, Bob Wyatt, Wayne Schafer, Ron Skillman, unidentified, James Irby, Kirby Black and Ken Killingworth. *Courtesy of Jack Best*

Jackson Junior High School, 1942. Front row, left to right: James Mann and Bob Hill. Second row: Laura Sausser, Ruta Armbruster, Lynnette Geiser and Donna Loffer. Third row: Gloria Doyle, unidentified, Lois Hottenroth, Elsie Sharp, unidentified, unidentified, Marilyn Kalk and the rest are unidentified.
Courtesy of Lynnette M. Galloway

Shirley Krebs, left, with her mother, Geneva Krebs, at 209 McDonough St., 1945. In the background are two pictures of Geneva's sons, Ray and Harvey, who were serving in World War II. *Courtesy of Sherri Dominick*

Westerhold family at Decatur Street, 1942, left to right: Andrew, Charles, Sophia and in the front is Jim. *Courtesy of Jim Westerhold*

Roland Beverick with his niece, Rita Rengel, in Washington Park, June 1942. Roland is home on leave from duty in the Coast Guard during World War II. *Courtesy of Rita Rengel*

Clayton Barrett, U.S. Navy, left, with Leo Roth, U.S. Army, at 1305 Prospect St., 1942. *Courtesy of Renee Barrett*

Arthur Sehlmeyer, on leave from the U.S. Navy, at his home at 618 McEwen St., January 1943. *Courtesy of Gary R. Mussell*

Collecting tires for World War II, circa 1943, left to right: Harry Hibbard, John P. LaFene and (unknown) Stevens. *Courtesy of Sue LaFene*

Fox Fisheries crew tarring nets at North Bass Island, August 1942. In the front row on the left is John "Puzz" Zura. On the truck in the foreground is George Hartlaub Sr., and on his left is Simon Fox. *Courtesy of Dale A. Hartlaub*

Weyer family at 1409 Camp St., 1945. Front row, left to right: Judy, Jerry and Jim. Back row: Ruth and Cletis. *Courtesy of Judy Hippler*

Juniors, sophomores and freshmen on Sandusky High School varsity football team, 1943. That year Sandusky High School did not play interscholastic football as a patriotic gesture to save gasoline and reduce unnecessary travel. Very few other schools followed this gesture; Sandusky resumed interscholastic competition in 1944. Front row, left to right: Jerry Blair, Jim Perrine, Bob Sprau, Jack Van Blarcum and Kon Bohannon. Second row: William Murphy, Carl Barnett, Leo Kohler, Myron Wilk, Chet Mischler and Leroy Downs. Third row: Wally Platte, Don Zimmerman, Dave Babcock, Tom Flippen and Jack Sloat. Back row: Jim Meckstroth, Maynard Nielson, Dick Beis and Joe Yost. *Courtesy of Walter Platte*

Lew Byington holding son Lew Jr. at 611 Perry St., June 1944. Lew served in World War II with the U.S. Navy Seabees. He later owned Lew Construction Co. and was a carpenter/contractor in Sandusky for 32 years. *Courtesy of Cherie James*

Left to right: Edwin E. Schultz, Jerry Schultz and Margie Dahm Schultz, 1945. Edwin was home on leave from the U.S. Army visiting his son and wife. He was stationed in the Philippines, where he was in charge of building air strips. *Courtesy of Julie Faetanini*

At the Erie County Service Organization (USO) Center, 1942, left to right: Peggy Schaufelberger, a sailor and Phyllis McDougall.
Courtesy of Peggy Scherer

Williams Accordian Band in front of Sandusky High School, circa 1944, Mr. Williams, front, far right, had a music store on Market Street. Virginia Schuh is standing behind him to his right. *Courtesy of Virginai Schuh Daniels*

First-grade class at St. Mary's School on Jefferson Street, 1944–45. *Courtesy of Jeanette Ruffing*

VFW float going north on Columbus Avenue during the All-Ohio Veteran's Day Parade, Aug. 3, 1946. The driver is Basil Glass, and the soldier on the far right is Richard Leitzke. *Courtesy of Virginia Bohn*

In front of Barkel's Ice Cream parlor, Madison and Fulton streets, 1947. Left to right: Jenny Mosser, Jim Gerold, Lois Brindley and Audrey Herb. *Courtesy of Jane Daniel*

Spalla brothers, left to right: Charles, Mario, Joseph, Salvatore and Anthony, circa 1945. All the brothers graduated from Sandusky High School and grew up at 1106 W. Washington St. They and their sister Frances were the children of Antonino and Vincenzina, who operated a small grocery store.

Courtesy of Anthony J. Spalla

City League Champions, 1946. Norm Hoelzer is on the left of the front row.

Courtesy of Barbara Kresser

Second graders at Perkins School, 1946. Front row, left to right: Chester Hiedle, Tom Mapus, Barbra H., Carol H., Dean Howman, Helen S., Bill Miller, Jim Decker, Albert Clark and Jerry Franketti. Second row: (unknown) Elford, Judy S., Wesley Dahm, Sharon Perry, Johnie W., Cora Roth, Doug Bruno, Donna Pukrin, Judy Olds and Judy Smith. Third row: Marietta DaGiau, Fred (unknown), Charles Hummel, Bobby H., Peter Zorn, Bobby F., Evon S., Maxine G., Carol P. and John W. Back row: teacher Mary Acierino, Carol W., Glen Kromer, Ray Dewelle, Judy Pratt, Donald Young, Mary (unknown), Joyce J., John Lenard and Alvin Nosthiemer. *Courtesy of Candia S. Howman and Marietta DaGiau Kamann*

Standing on Columbus Avenue are Marilyn Gast, left, with her mother, Wilma Gast, June 1947. *Courtesy of Brenda Bahnsen*

Sandusky High School cheerleaders, 1948–49. Left to right: Jim Huth, Arline Landin, Loretta Thiebert, Darline Landin and Tony Spalla. *Courtesy of James A. and Martha Bertsch*

Huron Elementary School first-grade class, 1946–47. Front row, left to right: Joyce Wasily, Wilma Franklin, unidentified, Carolyn Leidheiser, Joanne Dute, Connie Bacon and Margery McComb. Second row: Brad Bickley, unidentified, Jean Herber, Iris Bellamy, Judy Missioni, Janet Jensen, Marie Dellinger, Paula Hammond, unidentified and unidentified. Back: Joe Kidwell, Harold Brownell, Billy Hummel, unidentified, John Schenk, Jack Kokar, Paul Doyle, Gaton Chicotel, Dick Hartley and Bill Frye. The teacher is Mrs. Perhamus. *Courtesy of Aileen Hartley*

Second- and third-grade class at McCormick School in Huron, 1947. *Courtesy of Theodore M. Hinkle*

David Hartman on George "Gump" Hartman's threshing tractor in Berlin Township, 1949. *Courtesy of John Hartman and Ethel Smith*

Annual Christmas party for employees of the Pfanner Dry Cleaning Co. was held at Hotel Rieger, December 1948. Present at the party: Norbert Mehling, Kenneth Anglin, Henry Pfanner, Glen Welschenbach, Mrs. Douglas Harris, Doris Hartwig, Theresa Uhl, Clara Cornwell, Henry Hustedt, Herman Bryant, Frank Camella, Loretta Moosbrugger, Catherine Lipp, Rose Brennan, Alma Uhl, Mary Calabria, Mrs. Carl Dobrunz, Evelyn Leslie, Mrs. Lawrence Polta, Helen Smith, Alice Wiedman, Mrs. Albert Ritzenthaler, Mrs. Dewey Lacourse, Freda Manskey and Mr. and Mrs. Philip Pfanner. *Courtesy of Cherie James*

Mothers Federation Officers, 1948–49. Front row, left to right: Alice Hoelzer, Lucille Martin, Peggy Scherer and Mary Kay Zielske. Back row: retired president Ruth Holzhauser, Dorothy Malinovsky, Harriet Tanshon and president Helen Hill.

Courtesy of Peggy Scherer

Mixed chorus and the a cappella choir of Sandusky High School presenting The Seven Last Words of Christ at the Jackson Junior High School, 1948. *Courtesy of George L. Mylander*

Chartered bus trip to the Indians World Series games, 1948. They are at East Side Café on First Street.

Courtesy of Marsha Bennett Scott

Marilyn Schaefer, left, with daughter Gail at their home on West Mason Road in Monroeville, July 1949. Their house was an old one-room school that was moved down the road to a site next to the Schaefer farm.

Courtesy of Brenda Bahnsen

The 1950s

The fashions of the day included starched white shirts and skinny dark ties for men, and poofy dresses with below-the-knee hemlines for women, but we moved forward with the nation and brought new jobs and new opportunities to the area.

The Ford Motor Co. plant and GM's New Departure factory both opened by mid-decade, and those two manufacturers and all the associated businesses that sprung up to support them supported our economy and our lifestyles for decades.

A new high school opened on the edge of Sandusky in the hopes the city and Perkins Township would form a new governmental partnership and a partnership for education.

Downtowns sprinkled across the county in our communities served as the center of commerce and the center of our social lives. We worked harder, smarter and embraced changing technologies to become more efficient and prosperous as the decade rolled on.

Employees of J. C. Penney Company in downtown Sandusky, 1952. Virginia Schuh is in the front row, fifth from the right. The store was located downtown on Columbus Avenue. *Courtesy of Virginia Schuh Daniels*

St. Mary's basketball Protest State Tournament champions, 1950. They were the first area basketball team to go undefeated. Front row, left to right: Geo Kerber, Paul Keller, Jim Westerhold, Walt Wagner and Billy Weltlin. Back row: Bill Koelsch, Bob Kreidler, Tom Swint and Jim Smith. *Courtesy of Jim Westerhold*

Jeanne Crain receiving the key to Sandusky from Harold G. Schaeffer, ex-officio mayor, during the movie star's visit to the city in 1951. From left to right: Ernest Pascal, who authored more than 50 stories for the screen; Jerry Scholer of the Ohio Theatre; Jeanne Crain and Harold G. Schaeffer. *Courtesy of John and Alvina Schaeffer*

Sts. Peter and Paul School eighth-grade graduation, 1950. Front row, left to right: Bill Hartnett, John Carroll, Rosemary Incorvia, Nancy Jacalone, Rosemary Jacalone, Pat Devanna, Ray Rossi and David Steinen. Second row: David Gagnon, James Sabo, Marilyn Feagua, Pat Chimera, Josphine Caramagno, Peggy Tyler, George Hudson and Donald Gosser. Back row: Elaine Murray, Janet Bohn, Gloria Lester, John Campbell, Bob Garvin, Denny Platte, Peggy Morrow and Gail Granfield. *Courtesy of Walter Platte*

Christmas at the Krebs home at 1608 W. Madison St., circa 1953. Left to right: August, Kay on the horse and Rae Ann. *Courtesy of Sherri Dominick*

Margaretta High School varsity basketball team at Castalia, 1950–51. Front row, left to right: J. Keller, B. Kromer, G. Fitz, T. Gallagher and B. Bickley. Back row: T. Cattano, S. Kuns, C. Gallagher, R. Parcher, D. Rohrbacher, B. Lee and G. Moser. The coach is R. Skinner. *Courtesy of Marjorie Crecelius*

Choraliers at Sandusky High School auditorium, ready for the fall concert, 1950. Front row, left to right: Bob Dunne, Don Bohanan, Harry Meyer, Bob Hill, Jim Wichman, Jim Roesch and Jim Roberts. Back row: Jim Huth, Dick Meyer, Jim Mears, Jim Mann, Jean Hottmann, accompanist Bob Betz, Esther Lehman, director Wayne Harmon, Vern Michaels, Bob Wilke and Clare Kosbab. *Courtesy of Martha Barnhart and Jean H. Karbler*

Holy Angels first communion class, May 27, 1951. Front row, left to right: Jane Myers, Carol Williams, Sandi Michel, Carol Ann Dickens, Nedra Angus, Barbara Tomich, Toni Ward and Linda Dienes. Second row: Mike Maschari, Richard Kubitz, Paul Braun, Patrick Patterson, Craig McCloskey, Jimmy Butts, Michael Gerber and Alfred Gonthier. Third row: Vicki Fazekas, Beverly Laws, Mary Lou Faggionato, Ruth Ann Gruhlke, Mary Lou Noftz, Sharon Ryan and Mary Lou Corbin. Fourth row: Joyce Comeaux, Sue Teasel, Linda Biechele, Gerry Capucini, Ruth Albert and Tom Gerold. Back row: Ron McQuerey, Jerry Bonderer, James McElroy, Richard Mills, Bill Derrick and Paul Raab. *Courtesy of Barbara Ott*

Margaretta High School varsity cheerleaders in Castalia, 1949–50. In the front, left to right, are Virginia Sowder and Betty Williams. In the back row are Joan Kuns and Marjorie Fitz. *Courtesy of Marjorie Crecelius*

Jack Koegle, left with brother Dick on the train at Kiddie Land on Cleveland Road in Huron, circa 1953. *Courtesy of Dick Koegle*

First-grade class at St. Mary's, 1950. Front row, left to right: Thomas White, Thomas Smith, Michael Ball, Spencer Klucas, Duane Sartor, Bernard Pfefferle, David Holscher, Charles Schiefley, Thomas Rife, Thomas Polta, Michael Herb, Richard Weigal, David Ott, Dale Christman, Thomas Hillenbrand, Daniel Riedy, John Biehl, Eugene Sensback, Lloyd Nickle, Richard Harrison and James Corley. Second row: Sandra Gruhlke, Judith Myers, Mary Brown, Charlotte Faulhaber, Rae Ann Krebs, Rose Davis, Mary Sturbaum, Karen Blakley, Janet Borsick, Kathleen Geisler, Carol Michel, Barbara Fischer, Margaret Rose Coleman, Susan Koelsch, Ann Sumser, Jeanette Long, Marcia Meggitt, Margaret Green, Therese Groff and Mary Margaret Kromer. Third row: Donald Schippel, Jack Riedy, Anthony Kramer, Leonard Fritz, Richard Cann, Paul Tremmel, Dennis King, William Kaiser, Donald Kautz, David Reno, Arthur Gerold, Dean Stehle, Charles Kromer, Terry Kaman, Larry King, Michael Yeager, Jack Friedman and Dennis Bertsch. Back row: David Stein, Donald Harkelroad, Paul Graves, Carol Gundlach, Mary Sartor, Bonnie Carruthers, Sally Thom, Maureen Kelly, Rita Haas, Karen Renwand, Diane Mineo, Karen Geiger, Virginia Dennis, Sandra Maier, Suzanne Johnson, Alice Chamberlain, Doug Drouillard, Dennis Smith and Charles Stanley. *Courtesy of Barbara Ott*

Horse-drawn wagon at the Bellevue Cherry Festival Centennial Parade, 1951. *Courtesy of Ruth Zimmerman*

Sandusky High School football team, 1950. Carl Hallo, far left in the middle row, and George Kreimes, second from the left in the back row, were co-captains and All-Ohio players.
Courtesy of Sherri Dominick

Junior high school football team at McCormick School in Huron, circa 1950. Front row, left to right: John Sheets, Todd Lusher, Richard Leidheiser, James Hartley, Bill Wesley, Louis Sheetz, Larry Tische and Gerald Schnaitter. Second row: Al McMillian, Jack Wasily, Kenyon Auer, August Missioni, Jon Komerak, Jack Armstrong, Lehr Dircks, Donald Rhonehouse, Tom Long and Carl Cherry. Back row: Mr. Miller, Bill Harmon, Harold Skyver, William Hammond, David Orshoski, Leroy Brownell, Gary Everett, Tom Holland, Tom Griggs, Rollie Jackson, Raymond "Red" Lescher and Mr. Ag (unknown). *Courtesy of Theodore M. Hinkle*

Huron High School varsity basketball team, 1952–53. The team had a 15-2 record that year. Front row, left to right: manager M. Yahn, Leroy Brownell, David Meola, George Majoy, Charles Hutchison, Joe Taylor and Lester Brownell. Back row: coach Dick Klein, Jason Warren, Bill Handley, George Clements, Jim Armstrong, Tom Hartley and Loren Leidheiser.
Courtesy of Elizabeth Brownell

Ex-officio mayor Harold Schaeffer explaining the meaning of the newly-organized JACKS to Ann Rutledge and Henry Pfanner Jr., sixth-grade pupils at Monroe and St. Mary's grade schools respectively, circa 1950. JACKS stood for Junior Aid Conservation Klub.
Courtesy of John and Alvina Schaeffer

Knights of Columbus Roaring '20s dance at the Knights of Columbus home on Columbus Avenue, 1952. *Courtesy of Dr. John K. Schaefer*

Cutting wheat on Meadow Brook farm in Berlin Township, 1951. Catherine Hartman is riding the binder, and driving the tractor are John, left, and David Hartman. *Courtesy of John Hartman and Ethel Smith*

ABC's Chicago bowling team in Sandusky, 1953. Left to right: Al Hosfeld, Tony Nartker, Walt Matter, Coby Bennett, Del Tucker and Bob Coyle.
Courtesy of Marsha Bennett Scott

Sandusky track team, district runner-up, 1954. Front row, left to right: J. Drage, L. Alexander, D. DeHaven, P. Gallagher, M. Sharp, S. Webster, G. Glenwright and B. Shelton. Middle row: manager C. Pascoe, J. Warfield, J. Bettridge, L. Corso, L. Stowers, R. Klein, D. Didelius and G. Rhonehouse. Back row: Assistant Coach Tabler, L. Robbins, D. Routh, P. Murschel, R. Millar, E. Kelly, G. Dickman, B. Clark, H. Burger, J. Paullin, B. Whisner and Coach Weis. *Courtesy of Judith and Patrick Gallagher*

Diane Sehlmeyer behind her family's home at 1536 Pearl St., April 10, 1955. *Courtesy of Gary R. Mussell*

Mrs. Downing's first-grade class at Ohio Street School in Huron, 1953–54. Front row, left to right: Bartley Proctor, Larry Diebert, Norman Bostater, Donald Ramsey, Ronald Elmlinger, Richard Millis and Edward Haber. Second row: Jane Wile, Suzzanne Peltier, Tomma Slocum, Chris McCormick, Sandra Leidheiser, Marsha Noftz and GraceAnn Towne. Third row: Susan Swanbeck, Tommy Randall, Robert Slygh, Ricky Braun, Bobby Wright, Bryan Molnar, Billy Duffy and Virginia Doust. Fourth row: Michelle Schroeder, Geanne Bilger, Dean Smith, Marsha Gockstetter, James Sprague, Kay Zimmerman, Linda Cherry, Peggy Rosswurm, Della Zimmerman and Mrs. Leona Downing. *Courtesy of Merita Wright*

Eighth-grade class at McCormick School in Huron with teacher Mr. C. Moore, 1953. Front row, left to right: Patsy Majoy, Barbara Tracy, Janice Cook, Janet Thompson, Jean Ann Stout, Joan Bardshar, Marlene Osterling, Lois Ritzenthaler and Marjorie Light. Second row: Ruth Wade, Barbara Griggs, Susan Purvis, Louann Fox, Carolyn Klein, Martha Shoop, Margaret Nickles, Linda Frye and William Cool. Back row: Patrick Barett, Theodore Hinkle, Jack Armstrong, David Dahlhofer, Daniel Weager, Jack Wasily, Al McMillian, Larry Tische and Rolland Schlessman. *Courtesy of Theodore M. Hinkle*

A visit with Santa at LaSalles Store, December 1954, left to right: Santa, Tom Wright and Bob Wright.

Courtesy of Merita Wright

Mechanical's team won the New Departure plant softball title as first shift champions, 1953. They topped the Torno's, the second shift team, in the play-off. In front are umpires Fred Orr and Gill Harple. Front row, standing left to right: Vic Dienes, Don Benschoff, Joe Severance, Bob Beverick and Bill Alber. Back row: Dick Gruhlke, Charles Olsen, George Wood, Dale Cable, Frank Picato, Clarence Boytim and Paul Endle.

Courtesy of Marie Severance

Anne Lamb, three years old, swinging in Groton Township, 1954. *Courtesy of Anthony Schaefer*

Eighth-grade graduation at Sts. Peter and Paul Catholic School, June 6, 1954. Front row, left to right: Rosalie Jorger, Patricia Millott, Marietta DaGiau, Marie Centorbi, Sandra Smith, Francis Brown, Ruth Rieff and Judy Knauer. Second row: Anthony Caponi, Joe Barone, Sally McLaughlin, Margaret Lester, Sheila Stanley, Susan Thomas and Patricia Reedy. Third row: David Cross, Larry Koehr, Steve Olsen, David Robinson, Tom McCafferty, Jerry Franketti and Richard Opper. Fourth row: John Macina, Gary Kurtz, Joe Poggiali, Carl Grimani, James Johnson, Pat Murray, Jerry Murray, David Hoover, Tom Faber and Charles Catri.

Courtesy of Marietta DaGiau Kamann

Mrs. Frances Buell's kindergarten class at McCormick School at Ohio Street in Huron, 1954–55. Front row, left to right: Mike Skyker, Donald Cherry, Dale (unknown), Frankie Mount and Tommy Wright. Second row: Pat (unknown), Timmy (unknown), David Braun, Richie Burkett, Mike McMillen and Donald McMillen. Third row: Donna McMillen, Anna Wonder, Jane Hughes, Suzie Matt, Lana (unknown) and Patty (unknown). Back row: Jim Bilgen, Larry (unknown), Debbie S., Charlie (unknown), Tommy Routh and Danny (unknown).

Courtesy of Merita Wright

Suzanne and Dick Koegle in their homemade go-cart with brother Jack at McKinley Street, 1952. Jack is in a body cast recovering from a fractured femur. *Courtesy of Dick Koegle*

Sandusky district championship basketball team, 1954–55. Front row, kneeling, left to right: J. Harpst, B. Whisner, P. Gallagher, G. Glenwright, T. Murray, R. Lange and J. Engelsen. Standing in the back row: Coach Regan, C. Alexander, G. Miller, J. Hammond, B. Laird, S. Dickerson, J. Bettridge, J. Johnson and B. Fairfield.

Courtesy of Judith and Patrick Gallaghe

Second-grade class at Ohio Street School in Huron, Thanksgiving 1954–55. Mrs. Perhamus is the teacher. Front row, left to right: Sue Swanbeck, Kathy Macowitz, Bobby Wright, Donald Ramsey, Bobby Slygh and Tommy Randall. Second row: Chris McCormick, unidentified, unidentified, Tomma Slocum, unidentified and Charlene Matt. Third row: Craig Molnar, Linda Cherry Brian Molnar, unidentified, unidentified, unidentified and unidentified. Back row: Kay Zimmerman, Norm Bostuter, Della Zimmerman, Grace Towne, Peggy Rosswurm, Virginia Doust, Michelle Schroeder, unidentified and Graig Molnar.

Courtesy of Merita Wright

Family picnic at East Harbor Park, July 1954. In the front, left to right: Stevie Gast, Philip “Flipper” Gast, Jeff Wilken, Susie Schaefer, Kathy Gast sitting in the water and Gail Schaefer. Marilyn Schaefer is in the back. *Courtesy of Brenda Bahnsen*

Sandusky High School Blue Steaks, Buckeye Conference championship football team, 1954. Front row, left to right: J. Schwanger, S. Webster, L. Robbins, M. Pankow, D. Jagel, P. Gallagher, B. Lange, K. Loreno, C. Snowden, D. Nebergall and G. Bickley. Second row: R. Kiser, J. Miller, D. Daniels, M. White, J. Engelsen, L. Tight, J. Warfield, C. Frutig, J. Rehfuss, G. Kosbab, L. Stowers and J. Harpst. Third row: M. Gilmer, R. Dahs, Z. VanBarg, R. Kaufman, R. Wightman, L. Corso, T. Wood, A. Payne, B. Whisner, R. Unckrich and G. Buck. Back row: B. Laird, H. Burger, R. Mainzer, J. Bettridge, A. White, E. Kelly, K. Cousino, G. Jolliff, R. Everett, B. Clark and J. Wild.

Courtesy of Judith and Patrick Gallagher

American Crayon Company employees being recognized for 35 to 39 years of service.

Courtesy of John and Alvina Schaeffer

John David Trumpower on his Harley Davidson with niece Daria Graves on the back at Milan Road, 1959. *Courtesy of Clint A. Trumpower*

After church on Easter morning visiting their grandparents, John and Wilma Gast, at 1523 Camp St., 1956. Left to right: Brenda "Susie", Billy and Gail Schaefer. *Courtesy of Brenda Bahnsen*

Owner and employees of Maschari's Beverages, a Pepsi distributor, at Strobel Stadium, 1956. Left to right: Jimmy Maschari, Frank "Toots" Maschari, Bill Houser, Jim West, Michael Maschari and Bill Borden. *Courtesy of James A. and Martha Bertsch*

Sonny Lang's Texaco station at the corner of Strub and Milan roads, 1957. *Courtesy of Jack Best*

Sandusky Travel Service, located in Hotel Rieger next to the lobby, circa 1957, left to right: Aileen Slyker, Miriam Stimson and Nancy Grathwol. *Courtesy of Nancy Grathwol*

Providence Hospital School of Nursing capping ceremony for the class of 1959 at Sts. Peter and Paul's gym, March 5, 1957. *Courtesy of Jeanette Ruffing*

Ruth and Leo Gundlach at the service counter at their store, Gundlach Grocery, on the corner of Columbus and Cowdery streets, 1958.
Courtesy of Tom and MaryLou Gundlach

St. Stephen Evangelical and Reform Church on Lawrence Street, April 14, 1957. Front row, left to right: Linda Parker, Karen Bechtel, Arlene Branam, Marsha Bennett, Gail Hartenfeld and Paulette Endle. Second row: Thomas Wilke, Douglas Greene, Rev. Richard Belsam, Robert Handy Jr. and Donald Cane. Back row: Allan Timple, Duane Knauer, Jerome Flowers, Richard Acierto, Robert Tucker and David Brown. *Courtesy of Marsha Bennett Scott*

Second-grade class at South Campbell School on Campbell Street, Nov. 19, 1958. Darrell James is in the third row, sixth from the left.
Courtesy of Cherie James

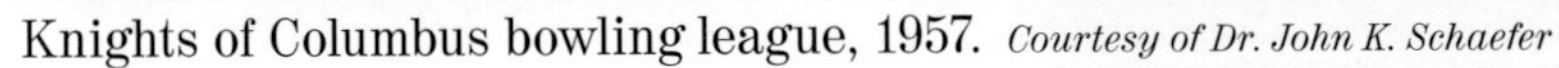

Knights of Columbus bowling league, 1957. *Courtesy of Dr. John K. Schaefer*

Sandusky native Pfc. Robert U. Keech serving in the U.S. Marines, January 1958.

Courtesy of Robert U. Keech

Second-grade first communion at St. Mary's School, 1959. The teacher is Miss Dubois. Front row, left to right: Anne Lamb, Sue Windau, Barbara Ruthsatz, Roseanne Cole, Shirley Schippel, unidentified, Ginger Geason, unidentified, Patty Miller, unidentified, Jane Burre, LeeAnn Ward and Carol Polta. Second row: Nick McCall, Steve Schippel, unidentified, unidentified, Christine Schnellinger, unidentified, Pat Coleman, Donna Kaman, Vicki Palmer, unidentified, Dan Brown, unidentified and unidentified. Third row: The first seven people are unidentified, Bob Hall, unidentified, Greg Christman, unidentified and Ed Windau. Fourth Row: Billy Cheatham, Michael Voltz, Joe Herold, Mike Sartor, Kathy Kromer, Father Inkrot, Karen Keller, unidentified, unidentified, Leon Groff and Jimmy Wensick. *Courtesy of Anthony Schaefer*

THE 1960S & '70S

The revolution continued, and starched white shirts began to give way to tie-dye T-shirts, alternative lifestyles and the peace movement.

As a nation and as a community we mourned the assassination of a young president, and later we mourned for his brother and for the great Civil Rights leader who led a transformation in society. We marched for peace in the streets and we marched for equal rights for all Americans. And many of us came to believe, for the first time, that the nation was involved in an unjust war while others stayed sure in their belief that a firm commitment would lead to victory in Vietnam.

The "Me Decade," as 1970s became known, brought more protests in the streets and the eventual downfall of a president. Our industries prospered in the good times, became leaner in the hard times and survived the recessions. In Perkins Township work began on the biggest building project to date, the Sandusky Mall, and a new business district was born.

After the crowning of Sandusky native and resident Jackie Mayer as Miss America 1963 in Atlantic City, New Jersey, Sept. 8, 1962. Left to right: Beth Mayer, Beverlie Mayer, Jackie Mayer, Jack Mayer and Jim Mayer.
Courtesy of Jackie Mayer

Candy and Jim Sharpe at their grandparents' home in Sandusky, circa 1960.
Courtesy of Candia S. Howman

Jim Wilken with his sons, left to right: Jeff, Mike and Pat. They are at their home in Bay View, circa 1960.
Courtesy of Brenda Bahnsen

Woolworth Co. fire at Columbus Avenue, Jan. 5, 1960. *Courtesy of Mary Steele*

New Departure employees gathered for the retirement of Mike Burch, 1960. Seated in the front, left to right: George Hahn, Bob Gast, Mike Burch, Freddie Miller, Howard Mahl, Sammy Kearns and Clarence Dalton. Second row: Warren Feiszli, Doug Moore, Martin Kinczel, Richard Quinn, Bob Beverick, Harold Kubach, Amil Johnston, Leo Stratton, Eddie Homes and Clarence Britt. Back row: Charles Coleman, George Moehlman, Rollie Zeck, unidentified, Bob Stevens, Ralph Dubbert, Richard "Hap" Folk, Art McCreedy, Joe Moran and Ray Zucker. *Courtesy of Sue Frankart*

At Cedar Point Beach, 1966, left to right: Carol Lippus, Sue Brackney, Barbara Erickson, Dolores Boitel, Shirley Barth and Mary Lou White. *Courtesy of Dolores Boitel*

"Ned's" bowling team at the American Bowling Congress Championship in Detroit, 1961. Left to right: Don Smith, Ned Tracht, Ed Schlett, Hubert Harrison and George Stahl. *Courtesy of John Hartman and Ethel Smith*

Ohio state baseball league in Kimball, 1960. Front row, left to right: Fred Dahs, Smitty Canterberry, Ken Nagle and Walt Long. Second row: John Bragg, Gene Dahs, Tom Bertsch, Jim Schaffer, Carl Brown and Ed Rease. Back row: Tom Rudolph, Jack Rue, Ed Roll, Jack Schaffer, Fred Lohmann and George Bickley. *Courtesy of John Bragg*

At 1217 First St., circa 1960, Lata Ritter with brother Rodger Hitchcock holding Lata's son Scott. Rodger, a paratrooper, was home on leave. *Courtesy of Mrs. William (Lata Hitchcock) Ritter*

Phillips 66 city league slow pitch softball team, 1960. Front row, left to right: Tom Rudolph, Hal Berger, Tom Bertsch, Walt Long and Butch Shilvey. Back row: Bill Arthur, Bob Row, Don Ebert, John Bragg, Ralph Summers, Eldy Andres, Bob Boos and Fred Dahs. *Courtesy of John Bragg*

Sandusky Sailing Club at the Battery Park dock, July 1961.
Courtesy of Tom and MaryLou Gundlach

Sandusky High School industrial arts teachers, Jan. 30, 1962. Front row, left to right: Edward Schilman, Edward Clark, William Wagner, Irwin Carpenter and Ray Riems. Back row: Jeff DeHaven, supervisor Dorwin Laessle, David Mackey, Vincent Madama and Donald Coe. *Courtesy of Elizabeth Riems*

Fourth-grade class at Meadowlawn Elementary on Strub Road in the Perkins School District, 1961–62. Front row, left to right: Mrs. Dorn, Doug Shaffer, Carol Ging, Emil Lang, Marilyn Pfefferkorn, Steve Zorn, unidentified, Gary Thompson and unidentified. Second row: unidentified, unidentified, unidentified, Jim Galloway, unidentified and Terry Andres. Third row: unidentified, Robert Popke, unidentified, unidentified, unidentified, Carlen Kenley, Denise Gettell, Don Stamm and Bonnie Bottger. Back row: unidentified, Phill Gastier, unidentified, Darrell James, Iola Pentorn, Randy Pendleton and unidentified.
Courtesy of Cherie James

Cousins at Christmas, 1962. Front row, left to right: Cindy Hoffman, Bobby Hoffman, Brian Callin, Denny Callin and Jeff Hoffman. Back row: Patty Hoffman, Susan Hoffman, Andy Hoffman, Jack Hoffman, Doug Hoffman and Bill Hoffman. *Courtesy of Sue LaFene*

Sycamore School at Sycamore Line, Jan. 22, 1964. Scott Ritter is in the front row, second from the left. *Courtesy of Mrs. William (Lata Hitchcock) Ritter*

McCormick Junior High in Huron with teacher Mr. Shoemaker, 1962–63. Front row, left to right: Charlene Kaman, Stephanie Armstrong, Fay Stoffer, Nina Murphy, Chris Craig, Dave Brown, Rex Edwards, Frank Ritter and Dave Wallace. Middle row: Suzie Hartley, Bonnie Bean, Ginger Browning, Duane Baun, Dave Braun, Bonnie Ross, Patty Emmert, Patty Ebert, JoEtta Crupi, Karen David and Sharon Napka. Back row: JoAnne Slyker, Sandi Brugler, Gail Lusher, Carol Evans, Cathy Ford, Bill Allendorf, John Zimmerman, Butch Allendorf, Jon Duffy, Mike Nealon and Kenny Lowry. *Courtesy of Karen David*

Vermilion Police Department, circa 1962. Allen Thompson is on the left in the back row.

Courtesy of Lynne Thompson Daughert

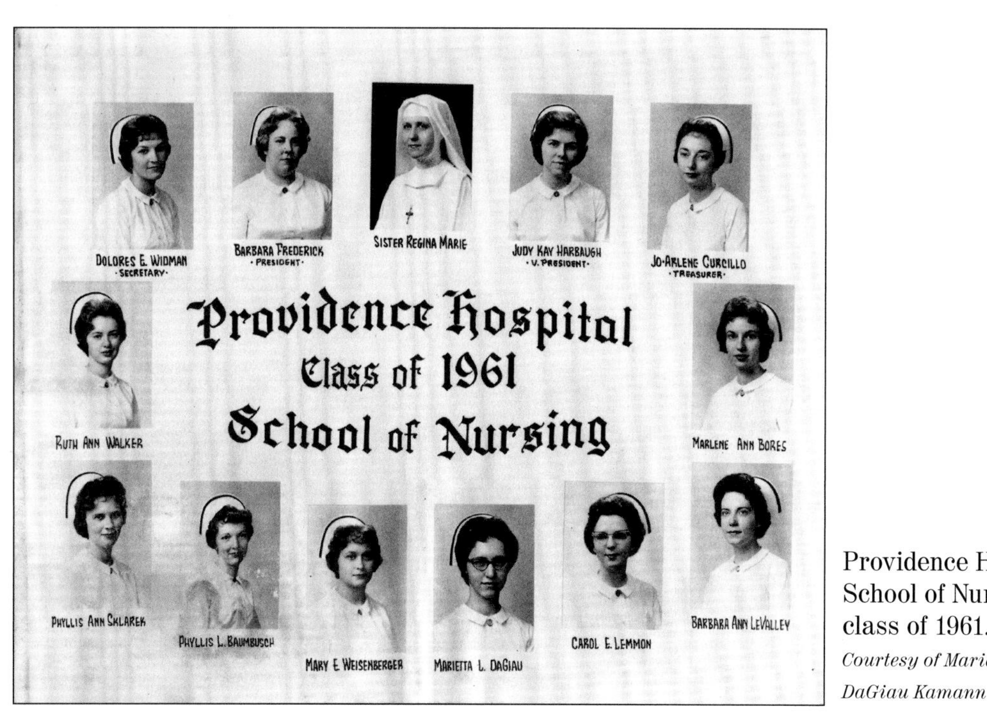

Providence Hospital School of Nursing class of 1961.

Courtesy of Marietta DaGiau Kamann

Seniors from Berlin Local School on a school trip to Washington, D.C., May 1963. Front row, left to right: Miss Purcell, Valerie Dixon, Beth Wright, Jane Bittner, Jackie Allen, Marie Holzhauser, Vickie Simonot and Patricia O'Brien. Second row: Rich Weaver, Carolyn Ward, Joanne Lonsway, Linda Kastor, Martha Palkovic, Liz Good, Pat Cooley, Frances Church, Janet Skiver, Melba Coughlin, Marianne Brod and Susan Smith. Third row: Mr. Sanders, Larry Cobb, Marshall Morgan, Patrick Dabrowski, Terry Plue, John Bobryk, Richard Hahn, Bruce Thayer, Larry Dute, John Leimaster, Roger Massey, Dick Koegle and Ron Johnson.

Courtesy of Linda Kastor Layton

Miss America homecoming luncheon at Sandusky High School, Oct. 30, 1962. Left to right: Jackie Mayer, Miss America; Fred Waring, leader of "Fred Waring and the Pennsylvanians;" and Dr. Lester Parker. *Courtesy of Jackie Mayer*

Hancock School third graders, 1964. Front row, left to right: Carolyn Hearn, Connie Vaccaro, Mike Francis, Tom Roberts, Ron (unknown), David (unknown), Sue Crabtree and Jake (unknown). Second row: Kathy Caffey, Calvin Bumpus, Linda Ohlemacher, Jean Balconi, (unknown) Dorsey, Kevin Jackson and Elsie (unknown). Third row: Eddie (unknown), Greg (unknown), Debbie Wobser, Patti Hibbard, Cheryl Byington, Sue Van Dootingh, Sue Seavers and Robert (unknown). Fourth row: Wade Brown, Pam Hartung, Carolyn Sanders, Sam Caffey, Melvin Reynolds, Linda (unknown) and Mike Weaver. *Courtesy of Cherie James*

Providence Hospital School of Nursing capping and lamp lighting ceremony, November 1966. Front row, left to right: Sister Catherine, Polly Jo Myers, Jan Coleman, Susan Molnar, Judy Opper, director Sister Jean Stack, hospital president Sister Lucia, Julia Reimer, Pat Ryan, Connie Edwards, Carole Suriano, Paula Ruffing and Betty Lehman. Back row: Gerri Skorupa, Margie Fife, Carlyn Lipke, Mary Lou Bauer, Marilyn Kancies, Susan Rine, Mary Sanders, Chris Beat, Linda Wagner, Sherry Alt, Pat Wagner, Ruth Schneider, Dorothy Schank, Deb MacRitchie, Jackie Garrard and Marsha Smith. In 2001, the school became Firelands Regional Medical Center School of Nursing.
Courtesy of Susan Rine

Ford tri-motor delivering mail and groceries at North Bass Island, circa 1966. *Courtesy of Dale A. Hartlaub*

Police bowling team recognized as league champs at the bowling banquet, 1968. In front, left to right: Mike Kresser, Lou Grathwol and Ted Goetz. Back row: Tom Coughlin, Bill Fox, Dave George, John Leffler, Del Seiler and Bob Grathwol. *Courtesy of Barbara Kresser*

First section of Cedar Point's new 330-foot Space Spiral Tower being cleared by customs inspector John J. Dutton at the Port of Sandusky, 1965. On the left is George A. Roose, Cedar Point executive; at right is Joseph Thompson of Norwalk Truck Line that hauled the 40,000-pound load from New York. *Courtesy of Jean Ward*

Erie County championship baseball team sponsored by Cameo, 1966. Front row, left to right: Joe Pankow, Monty Keech, Tony Sartor, Bruno Lizzi, Andy Anderson, Bob McLaughlin, Charlie Fresch and batboy Dan Sharp. Back row: (unknown) Zimmerman, John Harkeroad, Larry Kuns, unidentified, Charlie Keller, Jack Sharp and Sonny Herzog. *Courtesy of Robert U. Keech*

Supporting the St. Mary's High School basketball team on their way to the regional semi-finals in 1967. *Courtesy of Barbara Kresser*

Parade float honoring Sandusky High School and St. Mary's perfect season in football, Nov. 19, 1968. They were called the Dynamic Duo. *Courtesy of Michael J. Herb*

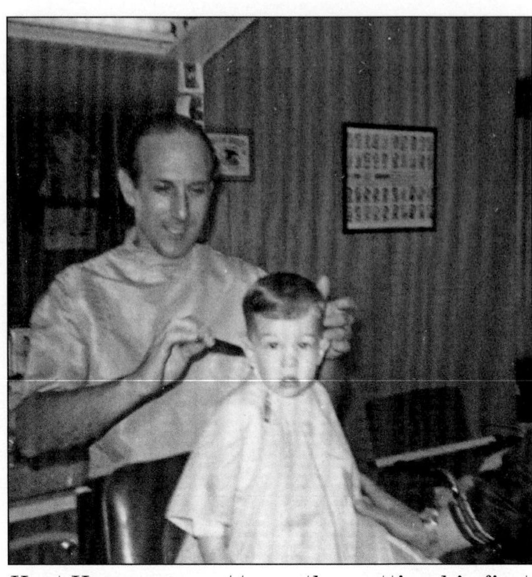

Kurt Kresser, age 11 months, getting his first haircut by Tony Damanti at his barbershop at Hayes Avenue Subway, May 6, 1968. *Courtesy of Barbara Kresser*

The Same Kind playing at Pony Tail teen club, October 1969. They traveled to Kentucky, West Virginia, Indiana and all over Ohio. Left to right: Gary Mazza, guitar; Bob Steele, bass guitar; Woody Wharton, drums; and Paul Ross, lead guitar. *Courtesy of Mary Steele*

Erie County Treasurer's Office staff at the Erie County Courthouse, circa 1969, left to right: unidentified, Betty Hartman, Virginia Grathwol, Mary Hennessy, Lucille Kniesel, Rosemary Fantozzi, Beverly Presslor and unidentified. *Courtesy of Janis Burke*

Clayton Barrett of Perkins Police Department, 1968.
Courtesy of Renee Barrett

St. Mary's High School majorettes, 1969. Ann Maschari is in front. Back row, left to right: Jackie Strasser, Christine Schaefer, Diana Martinez and Ann Shepherd.
Courtesy of Dr. John K. Schaefer

July Fourth flood of 1969 at the Camp Street Subway. *Courtesy of Ruth Zimmerman*

Aerial view of Vermilion during the 1969 flood. The boats were washed out to the lake. *Courtesy of Tom Root*

Senior Fellowship past-president and officers, circa 1970. Front row, left to right: Lou Franketti, Auggie Keumelle, Tom Young, Walt Platte and Earl Lonz. Back row: Foster Baker, A. Voight, (unknown) Bunge, L. Ebner, Jack Sharmon, George Davis, Clare Winston, Willard Jahraus, Earl Mischler, Mat Luberger, Pete Corso and Al Dorr. *Courtesy of Walter Platte*

Perkins Atom VFW League champions, circa 1970. Charles Ritter is in the front row, far left. *Courtesy of Mrs. William (Lata Hitchcock) Ritter*

Citizens Bank Classic League champions at Cedar Lanes, 1971–72. Left to right: Lennie Wyatt, Vito Dibari, George Tomich and Frank Fantozz. *Courtesy of Barbara Ott*

Cooper boys at Battery Park marina, 1971. *Courtesy of Joan D. Cooper*

State Fire School held in Sandusky at Fire Station #7, 1979. Sitting in front, left to right: Steve Ahlers, Tim Riester, John McGinnes, Don Troike and Tony Bonner. Second row: Howard Elgart, Bill Johnson, Keith Salinski, unidentified, unidentified, Pat Burns, unidentified, unidentified and Dean Howman. Third row: Jeff Ferell, (unknown) Urich, unidentified, Bill Hodges and unidentified. *Courtesy of Candia S. Howman*

Three generations of The Sandusky Paint Co. owners, 1978, left to right: Robert Wilke III, Robert Wilke and Robert Wilke II. *Courtesy of Dolores Boitel*

Dartball team representing East Side Café, 1975. Front row, left to right: Tony Schaefer, Tom Erne, Rich Wobser, Jack Erne, Rich Meyers and Chuck Obergerfel. Back row: Ken Lill, Commodore, Toby Notestine, Steve Kromer and Tom Kock. *Courtesy of Anthony Schaefer*

Installation of officers of Bethel #18 International Order of Job's Daughters, December 1979. Left to right: Laura Barney, guide; Lorinda Barnhart, senior princess; Kelley Blatt, honored queen; Linda Baird, junior princess; and Kathy Kurtz, marshal. *Courtesy of Martha Barnhart*

Elks bowling league at Cedar Lanes, May 1979, left to right: Gary Wahl, John Bragg, Ben Buser, Ned Brown and Paul Ruess. *Courtesy of John Bragg*

THE 1980S

In Ohio, we voted with most of the nation and brought a new brand of politics to Washington, D.C. With the landslide election of Ronald Reagan as president the modern conservative movement went into high gear.

The decade included hostile takeovers on Wall Street and Main Street. Downtown areas survived but did not prosper as the new business district along Milan Road in Perkins Township took root and continued to grow and grow, as farm fields gave way to development.

The Vacationland we always knew and loved also continued to grow, as Cedar Point built one awesome new roller coaster after another and the Northcoast became king of the coasters. Our industries survived against the new, hot competition from the Japanese, but they did not thrive. The seeds to bankruptcy in the American automotive industry were planted, but we did not know our way of life would one day change drastically as those seeds grew.

And we continued to chronicle our lives with every type of camera, from the film instamatics to the Polaroids that produced an instant photo at the click of the shutter.

Float in the Fall Festival parade on Kelleys Island celebrating the 150th Anniversary of Erie County.
Courtesy of Floren V. James

A typical day during cherry season at Pickett Cherry Farm, circa 1980. During World War II, German prisoners of war were brought in to help pick the cherries. *Courtesy of John and Alvina Schaeffer*

James Marshall driving his team of mules and wagon in a parade on Hayes Avenue, 1980. With the wagon are James Marshall, James Marshall Jr., Sabel Kopak, Shawn Kopak, Sandy Marshall, Judy Marshall and Hudson Marshall. *Courtesy of Rhett Marshall*

Mildred and Alfred Schnurr, circa 1980, on the beach across the street from their daughter, Janet Snyder's, home at 433 Cedar Point Rd. Alfred was the owner of Alfred Schnurr & Sons Construction Co. *Courtesy of Kim Seder*

Senior Golf League, YMCA, 1980. Front row, left to right: Harry Block, Al Baker, Walt Platte, Rockie Larizza, Harry Showalter, unidentified and Bill Keller. In back: Fred Hoffman, Harold Poulson, Lorne Buss, Al David, Alex Christoff, Glenn Ruh, Jim Solida, Ed Koezor, Homer Robinson, Al Schaeterle, Lou Behrender, H. Leassle, Ben Bickley, Alex Riesterer, Gil Barth, Ralph Otto, Don Ortner, Ed Firtch, Jack Wimer, Bob Glick, Bob Brenen, Rol Erney, Harry Archer, Harry Miller and Earl Carpenter.
Courtesy of Walter Platte

McGittigan Winery was built in 1867 on Kelleys Island. In the 1970s the building was purchased as the home of KIRA, Kelleys Island Recreation Association, owned by Mr. and Mrs. Floren James, Mr. and Mrs. Paul Leidheiser, Mr. and Mrs. Cloyd Dawley and Mr. and Mrs. Arthur Blackwell. *Courtesy of Floren V. James*

German Reformed Church on Division Street, Kelleys Island, circa 1980. Built in 1867, the building housed the Kelleys Island Historical Association in 2009. *Courtesy of Floren V. James*

Cecil Lamb, a Nickel Plate Road Engineer, operating his favorite Engine No. 765 at the Norfolk & Western Railroad Bellevue Yards in Groton Township, 1980. *Courtesy of Anthony Schaefer*

Ji Do Kwan Karate School at West Monroe and Vine streets, 1980, left to right: Dennis Bickley; his father, Brad Bickley; and Robert Cooper. Robert, owner of the karate school, was enshrined in the Ohio Karate Hall of Fame. *Courtesy of Bradley W. Bickley*

St. Mary's first communion class, 1982. *Courtesy of Barbara Ott*

Bringing the *G. A. Boeckling* home past Middle Bass Island, June 11, 1982. *Courtesy of Jean Ward*

Sandusky High School class of 1951 reunion at the Sandusky Yacht Club, 1986.
Courtesy of Dolores Boitel

Annual grandpa's day at Cedar Point, 1983. Front row, left to right: Jennifer LaFene, Jessica LaFene and Charity Hacker. Second row: Scott Hacker, Matt Deitz, Janel LaFene, Bob LaFene, Lynn LaFene and John LaFene. Back row: Karen Deitz, Bill LaFene, Cynthia Hacker and Paul LaFene. *Courtesy of Sue LaFene*

Angela Delius, daughter of Robert and Nancy Delius of 803 E. Fox Rd., summer 1982.
Courtesy of Rita Rengel

Erie County 4-H family campers on the rear stairway of the Ruggles Dining Hall on Kelleys Island, July 1983. *Courtesy of Roger L. Dickman*

Opening of the Rt. 2 Huron Bypass, 1980. They allowed foot and bike traffic before opening the road to cars and trucks. In front are Mary and Floren James; behind them are Ernest and Phyllis O'Hara. *Courtesy of Floren V. James*

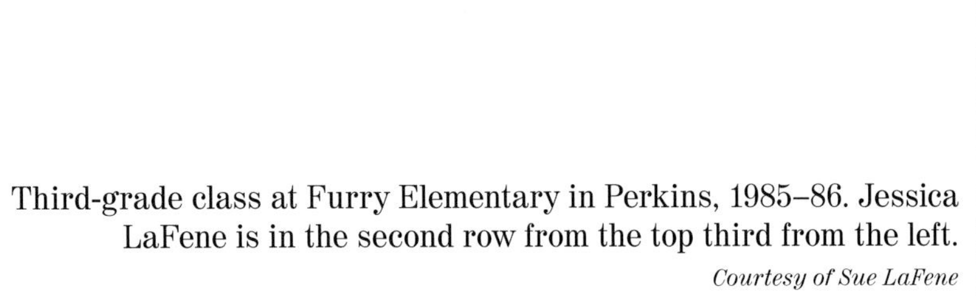

Third-grade class at Furry Elementary in Perkins, 1985–86. Jessica LaFene is in the second row from the top third from the left. *Courtesy of Sue LaFene*

New Departure Hyatt National Sales Conference attendees gathered on the #8 fairway at the golf course at the Sawmill Creek Conference Center, Huron, June 1983. *Courtesy of Doug Grubola*

Berlin Heights Little League baseball at Memorial Park, 1984. Front row, left to right: Kyle Ezell, Zach Eckel, Lucas Welch, Jeff Delamater and Chad Willgrubbe. Middle row: Scott Hayes, Rod Flowers, Scott O'Brien, Donnie Lewis, Zach Parsons, Jason Krisha and Jeremy Seck. Back row: coach Richard Eckel and Gene Seck. *Courtesy of Brenda Bahnsen*

Ninetieth birthday celebration for the Boy with the Boot statue, July 14, 1985. *Courtesy of Jeanette Ruffing*

Willard Grathwol, left, with Virginia Grathwol at Sawmill Creek Resort in Huron as she receives an award from Vern Riffe, Speaker of the House, on her retirment, Feb. 23, 1985. She was the first woman elected as Erie County Treasurer and served for 28 years. *Courtesy of Janis Burke*

Christmas at Strickfaden's Nursery on Bell Avenue in Perkins Township, 1985. The audio and animated Santa Claus was custom made in Germany. A visit to Strickfaden's was a Christmas tradition for many Sandusky area families. *Courtesy of Dona Ehrhardt*

Warehouse Managers meeting, NDH, June 1983. From left to right: Carl Eakes, Chuck Ryan, Gary Noblin, Bob Randel, Bill Kenney, Roger O'Halla, Doug Grubola, Paul List, Bob Gilmour, Jim Allen and Chuck Rowley. New Departure Hyatt was started in 1946. Prior to World War II, all the American bearing manufacturers were located on the East Coast. During the war, the fear of destruction from attacks to the shoreline prompted General Motors to open a new plant in Sandusky. The company had originally been based in Connecticut and New Jersey. New Departure started around the turn of the century producing the first brakes for bicycles. Hyatt began by making railroad bearings. The companies merged in the 1950s and moved their headquarters to Sandusky in the 1960s. *Courtesy of Doug Grubola*

The tall ship *Merkur* was brought in for viewing for the weekend at the Jackson Street Pier, September 1985. The *G. A. Boeckling* is in the background. *Courtesy of Michael J. Herb*

Arrival of the *M. V. City of Sandusky* from Louisiana to Battery Park Pier, 1986. *Courtesy of Candia S. Howman*

Newman Boat Line *Challenger* docked with a Newman Boat Line ferry in the background at the foot of Columbus Avenue, October 1986.
Courtesy of Michael J. Herb

Perkins School seventh-grade band, 1989. *Courtesy of Sue LaFene*

BPOE baseball team, 1985. First row, left to right: Dan Fredericks, Elmer Lippert, Fred Dahs, Terry Pitzer and Don Ebert. Back row: Tom Bertch, Walt Long, George Bickley, Ed Hartung, Gene Kidwell, John Bragg, unidentified and Gary Wahl. *Courtesy of John Bragg*

Perkins High School girls' cross country team in Osborn Park, 1987. Janel and Jennifer LaFene are fourth and fifth from the left. *Courtesy of Sue LaFene*

Beard contest at Kelleys Island Centennial, July 25–27, 1987. Left to right: Charlie Pascoe, Joel Feyedelem, Jim Kekelik, unidentified, Marshall Bokerman, Tom Kilbane, Wally Krzynowek and Claude Smith. Little John and Big Chuck were masters of ceremony. *Courtesy of Sandra Spayd-Kilko*

Kelleys Island Centennial celebration, July 1987. Each balloon sent off had a tag with a message to return a letter to Kelleys Island. Five were returned, one from Canada. *Courtesy of Sandra Spayd-Kilko*

Big Chuck, Little John and the clown lead the community to a balloon send off on Popeye's Deck as Kelleys Island celebrated its centennial during a three-day festival in July 1987. *Courtesy of Sandra Spayd-Kilko*

Swearing in of city commissioner Michael Kresser, 1986. His wife, Barbara, and children, Kurt, Chad and Marcy, are with him. He served in this role for 16 years. *Courtesy of Barbara Kresser*

Linda Schaffer, left, 1988 fair queen, with Jennifer Girard, 1987 fair queen, at the Erie County fairgrounds, August 1988. *Courtesy of Ted Schaffer*

At the Erie County fairgrounds, August 1989, left to right: Kelly Townsend, Jackie Mayer, Linda Schaffer and Beverlie Mayer. Kelly is the 1989 Pennsylvania fair queen and daughter of Jackie Mayer, the 1963 Miss America. Linda is the 1988 Erie County fair queen, and Beverlie is the mother of Jackie and one of the judges. *Courtesy of Ted Schaffer*

Byington family reunion at Singara Grotto on Campbell Street, June 2, 1988. The individuals are all descendants of Verne and Hilda Ebert Byington. *Courtesy of Cherie James*

Kelly Wilke on the carousel at Cedar Downs in Cedar Point, 1989.
Courtesy of Tammy Wilke

Band playing at the Kelleys Island Festival, 1988. The center trumpet player is John Blakeman. *Courtesy of Floren V. James*

Halloween on Memorial Drive in Berlin Heights, 1989. Front row, left to right: Holly Bragdon, Dawn Bragdon, Chelsey Eckel and Jordan Kastor. Back row: Zach Eckel and Daniel Kastor.
Courtesy of Brenda Bahnsen

Dante Zettler bags up a bottle of Glacial White wine for Rick Holmes at Kelleys Island Wine Company, 1989, in the original tasting room.
Courtesy of Sandra Spayd-Kilko

Erie County fair queen, Linda Schaffer, at the Fourth of July celebration in downtown Sandusky, 1989. *Courtesy of Ted Schaffer*

Four PT boats on location for the weekend at Battery Park next to Damon's, August 1989. Tours through the boats were offered to the community.

Courtesy of Michael J. Herb

Car show at Sandusky Plaza Shopping Center, June 1989.

Courtesy of Michael J. Herb

Sea Raiders semi-pro football team, 1989. Chad Kresser is in the front row, fourth from the right. *Courtesy of Barbara Kresser*

THE 1990S

A tempered decade, our industries continued to struggle but survived as thriving families worked hard and played hard.

We sent local soldiers to serve in the first Gulf War, and celebrated the victory and the technologies that changed how wars are fought.

How we played also changed with the introduction of the Super Highway. The Internet made everything different from how we interacted to how we shopped. Life took on a quicker pace as we grappled with the challenges of changing technologies and changing competition.

The term "Rust Belt" gained a secure place in our language as we saw the state and our community lag behind every economic recovery that took hold in other parts of the country.

St. Stephen Kiddie College, 1997–98. Mrs. Essex and Mrs. Keith were their teachers. Lynze Daugherty, wearing a black jumper and white blouse, is in the back being held by Mrs. Essex. *Courtesy of Lynne Thompson Daugherty*

Carriage ride in downtown Sandusky on West Washington Row, circa 1990. Carriage rides were available on weekends throughout the summer.
Courtesy of Michael J. Herb

Girls' league softball at Berlin Heights Memorial Park, 1990. Front, left to right: Chelsey Eckel and Kristen Salmons. Second row: (unknown) Myers, Michele Denny, unidentified, Wendy Laughlin and Tabby Myers. Coach Denny is in the back. *Courtesy of Brenda Bahnsen*

Homecoming queen, senior Jennifer LaFene, in the Homecoming Parade in Perkins, 1990. *Courtesy of Sue LaFene*

Heather Grubola, 1991 Huron Water Festival Queen, on Cleveland Road, July 1991. In 1992 the celebration was renamed the Huron River Festival.
Courtesy of Doug Grubola

Steam locomotive, Norfolk & Western Railroad's famous "J 611" that headed an excursion train taking passengers to the Ohio State Fair in Columbus, August 1991. *Courtesy of Michael J. Herb*

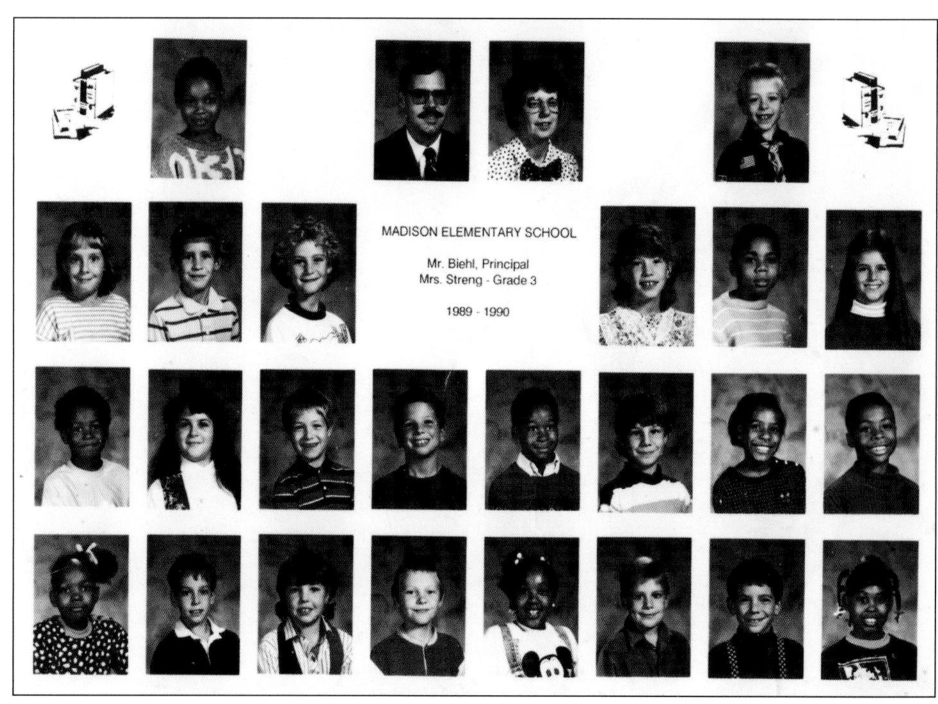

Mrs. Steng's third-grade class from Madison Elementary School, 1990. John L. Seder III is second from the left in the second row. The school closed in 2009. *Courtesy of Kim Seder*

Charles "Red" Carmen and his combo playing in the gazebo at Washington Park, July 4, 1991. *Courtesy of Joan D. Cooper*

The Robert and Joan Cooper family in Washington Park on July 4, 1991. *Courtesy of Joan D. Cooper*

Aerial view of downtown Milan during the Melon Festival, Sept. 1, 1991. *Courtesy of Tom Root*

Homecoming court at Perkins High School, 1992. Front row, left to right: Beth Myers, Ann Riccelli, Becky Mehling, Shannon Dubbert, Allison Terry, Rachael Fisher and Tracy Rose. Back row: Chris Wingader, Rick Nelson, Tim Ott, Jeff Lippus, John Voight and Jason Hermes. *Courtesy of Barbara Ott*

Perkins High School girls' track team, 1993. They were state bound qualifiers. Front row, left to right: Sarah Bickley, Angie Satterfield and Karla Hauser. Middle row: Nikki Litz and Nikki Sturzinger. Back row: Laura Yunghans, Jessica LaFene, Shelly Swain, Stephanie Hall, Sarah Wechter and Lisa Manuella. *Courtesy of Sue LaFene*

Tenth birthday party for Kristina Seder at the Seder home at 603 W. Washington St., Sept. 10, 1992. Kneeling in front are Annie and Ella Birli. Second row, left to right: Abby Lochotski, Bethany Davis, Kristina Seder in the multi-colored shirt, Anna Wilkinson behind her and Melissa Graves. Back row: Marcia Twyman, Jane Orafu, Julie Shaw and Monica Gill. *Courtesy of Kim Seder*

Edison High School freshman football team in Milan, 1992. Front row, left to right: Joe Taylor, Zach Eckel, Craig Mesenburg, unidentified, Cory Griffin, Phil Thayer and Charlie Rew. Middle row: Brian Smith, Adam Strong, Scott Jones, Adam Davis, Jason Utter, Jesse Mc Cullough and Pete Sax. Back row: coach Doug Crooks, Craig Lytle, Nate Kuhl, John Haueptle, Glenn Stieber, Jay Woodyard, Tony Leimeister and coach Chris Wert. *Courtesy of Brenda Bahnsen*

Confirmation class at St. Stephen United Church of Christ, 1993. Front row, left to right: Sarah Bittinger, Heather McGee, Andrea Nappi and Cari Miller. Second row: Pastor Novak, Greg Egbert, Gary Gochenour, Kendra Hand and Shane Toccaceli. Back row: Lindsey Hartung, Larry Balduff, Jason Ross, Marcia Braun and Pastor Shedlock. *Courtesy of Janis Burke*

Aerial view of Middle Bass Island airport, July 19, 1992. *Courtesy of Tom Root*

YMCA flag football players, 1994. In the second row on the left is Zachary Daugherty; on the right is Samuel Thompson. *Courtesy of Lynne Thompson Daugherty*

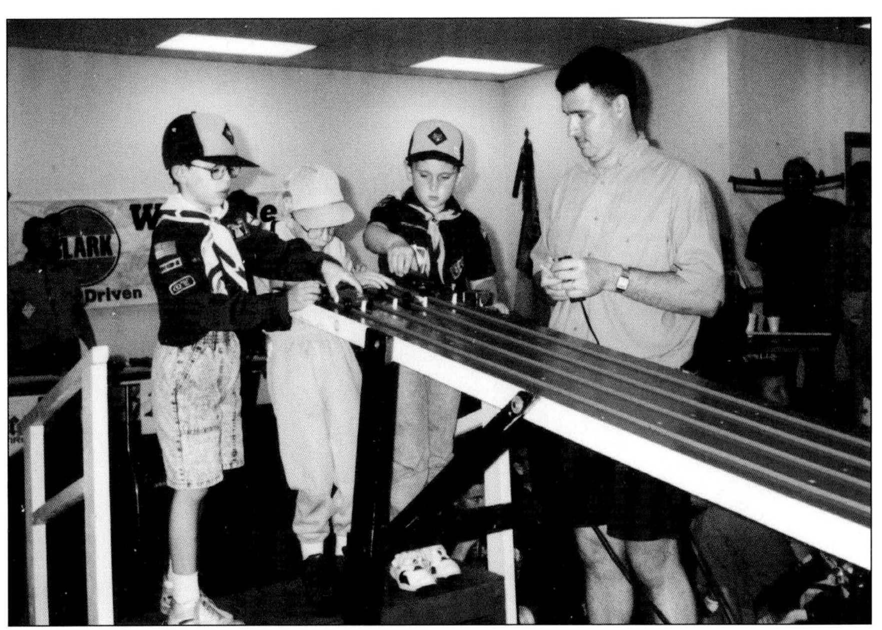

Cub Scout Pinewood Derby district race at the Outlet Mall in Milan, May 21, 1994. Joshua Schwanger is third from the left. *Courtesy of Donna Greene*

YMCA preschool, 1994–95. Front row, left to right: Ms. Lisa Nemeth, Kaitlyn McGooky, Michael Baxter, Jonathan McGookey, Jared Cullen, Allen Baum and Christopher Baxter. Second row: Kaitlyn Nemeth, Ashley Becker, Faith Young, Amber Trammell, Rachel Green, Emily Pankratz, Lea Kuns, Alyssa Aceto, Kristina Koch, Ms. Heather Walton and Erin Baron. Third row: Ms. Janet Dahlgren, Tyler Dix, Christian McGory, David Ruff, Zachary Perdue, Benjamin Higgenbotham, Brandon Slater and Kevin Bauer. *Courtesy of Barbara Ott*

At Cedar Point, 1994, left to right: Janel LaFene, Jessica LaFene, Ester Veldboer and Rob Follaud. *Courtesy of Sue LaFene*

Caryl Crane and Jackie Mayer at the "Welcome Home Jackie Mayer" event, October 1997. Caryl Crane was known as Sandusky's "First Lady of Fashion." *Courtesy of Jackie Mayer*

Homecoming court at the Perkins High School track and football field, 1994. Queen Laura O'Neal and senior attendant Jessica LaFene are fourth and fifth from the left. *Courtesy of Sue LaFene*

St. Mary's High School class of 1961 celebrating their 35th reunion at Plum Brook Country Club, 1996. *Courtesy of Barbara Ott and Barbara Kresser*

Perkins High School girls' cross country team, 1994. Sitting in front, left to right, are co-captains Jessica LaFene and Stephanie Hall. Front row: Emily Eiselstein, Angie Satterfield, Polly Young, Beth Myers and Missy Etchill. Second row: Heather Schaefer, Beckie McEowen, Kate Higgins and Angie Jarret. Back row: Erica Kessler, Becky Stephenson, coach Chris Green, Jessica Blair and Diane Miller. *Courtesy of Sue LaFene*

Edison High School baseball team in Milan, 1995. Kneeling in front, left to right: Nate Kuhl, Zach Eckel, coach Mark Matula, Brad Simon and Jimmy Roe. Standing in the middle row: coach Shayne Fischer, Ben Gammie, Jake Deehr, Jeff Finnen, Jon Houser, Sam Springer and Jay Woodyard. Back row: Brian Booth, Coach McConnell, Josh Goodwin and Nick Gaudiello. *Courtesy of Brenda Bahnsen*

YMCA baseball team, June 1995. Front row, left to right: Brett Fuqua, Patrick Keeley, E. J. Keelem, Patrick Freeh, Scott Manuella, David Ruff and Miranda Hiss. Second row: Brett Fuqua, Matt Weiss, Brandon Slater, Natalie Reddaway, Katie McBride, Karl Fleck and Tim Fleck. Back row: Duke Slater and John Reddaway. *Courtesy of Barbara Ott*

Riedy and Weyer family reunion at 5610 Debra Dr. in Castalia, 1996. Front row, left to right: Judy Hippler, Jerrod Weyer, Heather Riedy, Nate Zitner, Ryan Riedy and Megan Zitner. Middle row: Darcy Riedy, Linda Chill, Sandy Zitner, Dorothy Riedy, Melvin Riedy, Jean Rader Miller, Shannon Chill and Jen Weyer. Back row: Lori Riedy, Vern Chill, Dick Riedy, David Zitner, Dan Riedy, Jerry Weyer, Betty Weyer, Jack Weyer, Carol Weyer, Bob Hippler and Lisa Hippler. *Courtesy of Judy Hippler*

Friends in the Sandusky High School Marching Band preparing for a Friday night football game halftime show, 1996. Left to right: Jonathan Adkins, Jennifer Bravard, Sirka Westgate, Andrea Faetanini and Michael Garner. *Courtesy of Julie Faetanini*

Girls' softball team at the shelter in Edison Park, Milan, 1996. Sitting in the front row, left to right: Rachel Enderle, Cassie Keefer, Chelsey Eckel and unidentified. Back row: Christy Shover, Gina Carnal, Allison Brauchler, Alison Muthig and Dawn Braden. *Courtesy of Brenda Bahnsen*

Sandusky High School baseball Erie Shore Conference champions with a 12-9 season, 1996. Front row, left to right: Derek Gangluff, Matt Wilken, Kirk Fortier, Shanan Aaron, Scott Deming, Jason Herb and Josh James. Back row: coach Tom Kowaleski, Chuck Willinger, Nile Sims, Jason Randleman, Matt Martin, Darcel Irby, Mike Lemons, Wes Kaufman and coach Bill Deming. *Courtesy of Cherie James*

Kroger Store cashiers raising $3,051.00 for Muscular Dystrophy Association, March 1996. Front row, left to right: Donna Andres, Debbie Blakely, Diane Lindsey, Jon Dubois, Ken Noser, Roz Rentz and Judy Hippler. Back row: Connie Salisbury, Betty Weyer, Lisa Vince and Monte Erwin.

Courtesy of Judy Hippler

Kris and Brandon Slater at Washington Park, July 4, 1997.

Courtesy of Barbara Ott

Edison High School varsity baseball in Milan, 1996. Front row, left to right: Sam Springer, Brad Simon, Ben Gammie and Jim Roe. Second row: Jeff Finnen, Jake Deehr, Jon Houser and Nick Gaudiello. Back row: coach Mark Matula, Dan Bibb, Nate Kuhl, Josh Goodwin, Zach Eckel and Brian Booth. *Courtesy of Brenda Bahnsen*

Student council at Berlin-Milan Middle School in Berlin Heights, January 1997. Front row, left to right: Dan Soisson, Katy Sisson, Philip Amstutz, Phil Fernandez, Cliff Hahn and Bobby Kandell. Back row: December Wikel, Chris Ruby, Julie Roberts, Chelsey Eckel and Amy Lewis. *Courtesy of Brenda Bahnsen*

German visitors sampling wine at Mantey Winery bar, October 1997. At the bar, left to right: Karl Heinz Weichel, Trautchen Pohlman, and Bob Weichel from Sandusky, Gustel Beumer and Fred Revering. *Courtesy of Bob Weichel*

Ninetieth birthday party for Alfred Schnurr at the Parkvue Nursing Home, Perkins Township, circa 1997. In front, left to right: Joey Seder, Alfred Schnurr, Jacob Cullen, Emily Lauber, Anne Rodriguez, Arianne Rodriguez and Francis "Bud" Schnurr. Standing: Ellie Schnurr, Joyce Cann, Kim Seder, Jim Mantey, Janet Kerber, Ron Schnurr, Connie Schnurr, Mary Ellen Cullen, Fred Kerber, Rebecca Cullen, Sarah Shaw, Rosemary Mantey, German Rodriguez, Kristina Seder holding Tony Rodriguez and John Seder.

Courtesy of Kim Seder

First communion at St. Mary's Parish, May 4, 1997. Zachary Daugherty is in the third row, fifth from the left.

Courtesy of Lynne Thompson Daugherty

Adams Junior High School football team, undefeated under head coach Ed Spayd, at a park on Huron Avenue, 1997. Included on the team: Ryan Baker, Chuck Crawford, Ryan Forney, Mike Griffiths, Brad Hall, Jon Heath, Matt James, Danny Johnson, Julian Johnson, Mark Miller, Mike Myers, Dustin Naylor, Malcom Ott, Ed Pool, Justin Randolph, James Saylor, Robert Smith, Travis VanDootingh, Dennarius Walk and Joe Work. *Courtesy of Cherie James*

Sandusky High School Marching Band at the Ohio Veterans Home Memorial Day parade, May 1997. Drum line, left to right: Andrea Roth, Andrea Faetanini, Scott Poeschl, Jessica Samko, David Henry and Nick Stacey. In front of them are Dennis Alexander and Matt Krafty. *Courtesy of Julie Faetanini*

Erie County Home Builders tournament, circa 1998, left to right: Ralph Henry, James Bertsch, Robert Fisher and Scott Fisher. *Courtesy of Robert Fisher*

Sandusky High School volleyball team after winning the first championship in the school's history, Oct. 15, 1998. Front row, left to right: Jen Gangluff, Mandi Miller and Khaisha Alexander. Middle row: Krista Neill and Kelly McCormick. Back row: Josie Niehm, Jeannette Dubois, Kenya Graves, Amanda James and Julie Shaw. *Courtesy of Cherie James*

Wilber family celebrating with their two girls after the Huron volleyball team won the state championship, 1999. In front is player Sarah Wilber. Behind her is her grandmother, Barbara Wilber. Standing, left to right: uncle Chris Harlan, mother Judy Wilber, player Janet Wilber, aunt Becky Harlan and aunt Dee Hartley. In back is their father, Dave Wilber. *Courtesy of Barbara Wilber*

VFW baseball team in the Memorial Day Parade in Perkins Township, 1998, left to right: coach John Stock, Nathan Barrett and Zack Hanacek. *Courtesy of Renee Barrett*

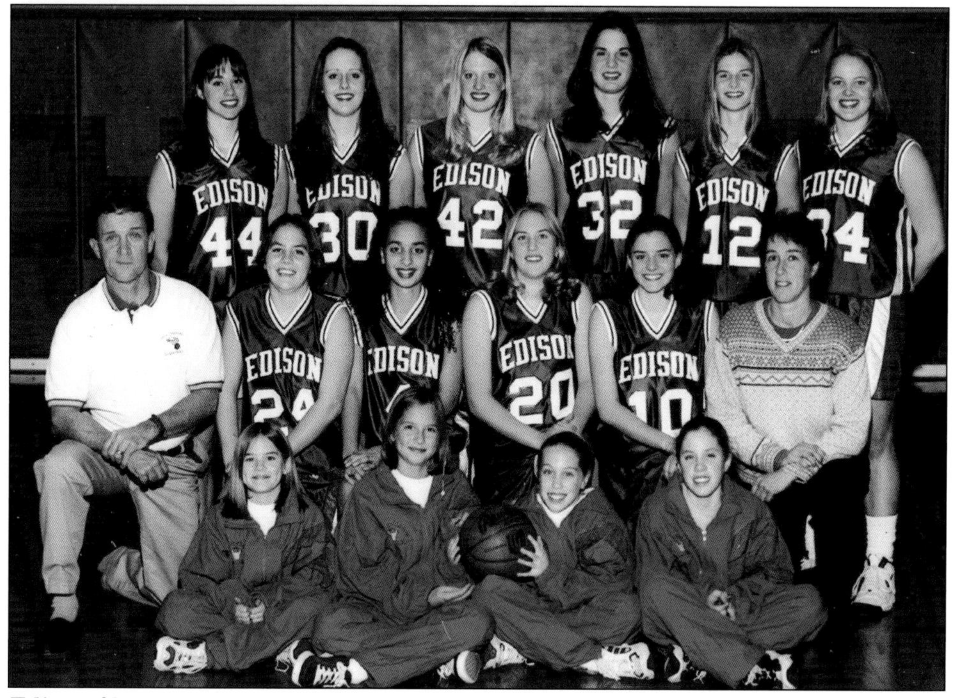

Edison Chargers girls' basketball team in Milan, 1998–99. Front row, left to right: Stacey Lewis, Michaela Christoff, Sarah Foster and Alex Wasco. Second row: coach Jim Colwell, Michelle Cochran, Erica Woods, Chelsey Eckel, Amy Lewis and coach Brenda Friend. Back row: Stephanie Moyer, Kelly Finnen, Kim Pifer, Megan Zitner and Julie Finnen. *Courtesy of Brenda Bahnsen*

A New Century

The dawn of a new millennium included "Y2K" fears, created when the experts told us the computers people and businesses had come to rely upon would crash a moment after midnight on Jan. 1, 2000. That disaster never occurred, but on Sept. 11, 2001, the nation mourned the deadliest attack in its history.

Nothing would ever be the same, and the attacks once again led us to send our young men and women to serve in a Gulf war, and this time there were casualties. We mourned the deaths of seven fallen sons from local families, and we supported them in their grief.

And our economy continued to struggle with the disappearance of thousands of manufacturing jobs as factories closed, and what many thought could never happen did, as General Motors declared bankruptcy and the American automobile industry, as a whole, slid toward insolvency.

As a community and as a nation, we have faced hard times before and survived to thrive. It's the American spirit that drives us.

Gundlach family at the Maxair ride at Cedar Point, July 17, 2005, left to right: Liam, Jordan, Zachary, Riley, Jacob, Molly, Carly and Morgan. *Courtesy of Tom and MaryLou Gundlach*

Beverlie Buck Mayer, Erie County Senior Queen, at the Ohio Veterans Home, 2000. *Courtesy of Jackie Mayer*

Schade-Mylander Plaza on the waterfront was dedicated Aug. 8, 2000. *Courtesy of George L. Mylander*

St. Mary's Boy Scout Troop 7 marching in the Memorial Day parade on Milan Road, 2000. *Courtesy of Donna Greene*

Jim Holzmiller's baseball team, 2000. In the front row, the first boy on the right is Dustin Holzmiller. In the back row, fourth from the left is Daniel Daugherty. *Courtesy of Lynne Thompson Daugherty*

Fiftieth reunion of the Sandusky High School class of 1950 at the Sandusky Yacht Club, September 2000. Seated on the floor, left to right: Pat Piper, Jean Lippus, Kit Karge, Betty Eickermann, Connie Cheshier, Sue Trueman, Jean Trumpower, Joyce Bouy, Don Winkel, Fred Fosco, Wilma Fanning, Harold Baaske, Caroline Gerber and Harold Koehler. Sitting in the second row: Peggy Perry, Norma Lorenz, Carl Hallo, Olive Henretty, Mary Lou Kopp, Joyce Sandersen, Katie Maschari, Katie Joss, Mary Kromer, Shirley Kaufman, Jane Garries, Tom Rotsinger, Tony Damanti, Nancy Heiler, Maxine Fraser and Ardeth Frye. Standing in the third row: Pat Bahnsen, Rosalie Krueger, Marilyn Liphart, Marilyn Speir, Nancy Yenney, Norma Japsen, Florence Yontz, Ray Nemitz, Arvilla Ulmer, Jean Lublow, Thelma Simmons, Shirley Robison, Mary Ann Schumacher, Marilyn Barbour, Mary Angello, Pat Stonerook, Shirley Barkan, Sharon Scheifley, Janis Werner, Barbara Borsick, Ann Dilgard, Ellie Schnurr, Nancy Harpst, Mary Jean Ellsworth, Nancy Sausser, Beverly Mears, Anne Missione, Don Hipp, Barbara Biechele, Dick Rankins, Carl Kusser, Angelo Giovagnoli, Tony Guerra, Gerri Krawetzki, Barbara Pfefferkorn, Gloria Spore, John Stevenson Jane Gerold, Hugh Lange and Eugene Dahs. Fourth row, first row risers: Carolyn Sizemore, Peggy Jamison, Arlene Stierhoff, Kathleen Rudiger, Marilyn Hornbeck, Sandra Dominick, Virginia Beuthel and Paul Ruess. Fifth row, second row risers: Anita Kibbee, Joan Groesch, Rita Guerra, Neil Lippus, Dave Waterfield, Shirley Baxter, Dick Grundler, Don Cottey, George Kriemes and Pete Lococo. Sixth row, top row risers: Carl Toft, Ben Elfers, Glenn Miller, June Roll, Charles Rickertsen, Ed Todd, Jim Henkelman, Bill Opie, Frank Dahlke and Dean Marr. *Courtesy of Mary Steele*

Canoeing on the Huron River between Huron and Milan at Erie MetroParks' Coupling Reserve, a train-themed park with canoes and authentic train cars available for overnight stays, Aug. 2, 2000. *Courtesy of Erie Metro Parks*

Theodore Tugboat visiting Sandusky at Meigs Street Pier, 2001. *Courtesy of Barbara Kresser*

Jean and Emery Ward Jr. in front of their collection of 1936 Fords at the Ford plant in Margaretta Township. Mr. Ward began searching for and restoring the cars, some from just rusted frames, in 1994. *Courtesy of Jean Ward*

Red Carmen, musician, performing in the gazebo at Washington Park, 2002. *Courtesy of Dr. John K. Schaefer*

Edison School homecoming in Milan, 2001. Front row, left to right: Tracy Maloney, Katy Sisson, Ashley Day, Chelsey Eckel, Gretel Meyer and Becky Poyer. Back row: unidentified, Chris Ruby, Kevin Lake, Jordan Kastor, Mike McCombs and Josh Kinney. *Courtesy of Brenda Bahnsen*

Edison High School seniors at the Milan Melon Festival egg tossing contest, Labor Day, 2001. On the left, front to back: Phil Amstutz, Bobby Kandell, Phil Fernandez and Chelsey Eckel. On the right: Danielle Springer, Emily Stoll, Becky Poyer and Kyle Meagrow. *Courtesy of Brenda Bahnsen*

Fiftieth class reunion of Margaretta High School at McClain's restaurant, Aug. 22, 2001. Seated, left to right: Bob Puchalski, Paul Kuebeler, Don Roggerman, Tom Davenport, Tom Baker and Max Bohn. Back row: Charles Dowming, Marlene Linkenback O'Dair, Mary Lou Gast Baker, Pat Keller Hofstatter, Ilene Hassinger DeWalt, Virginia Miller Lutes, Gladys Sessler Howell, June Stanley Thomas, Marge Fitz Crecelius, Jean Hoffman Fitz, Joan Kuns Crawford, Jane Hoffman Perry and Bonnie Richards Vargo. *Courtesy of Marjorie Crecelius*

Sandusky Womens' Bowling Association Board of Directors on the organization's 75th anniversary, 2001. Included are Yvonne Mason, president; Marie Severance, vice president; Ida Kusser, secretary; and Sharon Carpenter, treasurer. *Courtesy of Marie Severance*

Muratori family Relay for Life team at Perkins High School, 2002. From left to right: Mary Conry, Marlene Corso, Norma Scally, Barb Kresser, Carol Howell, Pam Canino and Pat Best. The girl in front is Madison Baum. *Courtesy of Barbara Kresser*

Amvets baseball team, 2001. Zachary Daugherty is second from the left in the front row. *Courtesy of Lynne Thompson Daugherty*

Annual wooden boat festival at Huron Boat Basin, August 2002. The old Eastern States Farm Exchange Mill is on the upper left. *Courtesy of Bob Weichel*

Edison High School boys' cross country team at the Tiffin Cross Country Carnival race, Sep. 7, 2002. Left to right: Nate Zitner, Curtis Barron, Ken Church, A. J. Hart, Clark Garris, Alex Ludwig, Greg See, Jon Sutter, Rich Koegle and Dan Weaver. *Courtesy of Julie Mingus Koegle*

High school prom-goers in front of the Boy with the Boot fountain in Washington Park, May 10, 2003. Left to right: Holly Blanton, Jacob Pawlowski, Joe Whelan, Lauren Sennish, unidentified, Steve Ferber, Joshua Schwanger and Victoria Lawrence. *Courtesy of Donna Greene*

At the Sandusky State Theatre Follies, Sept. 13, 2003, left to right: Jean Karbler, Judy Mears, Dr. Harry Stenzel, Laura Stellhorn and Jean Bossetti. Dr. Stenzel played the butler in the "Gone with the Wind" segment as the others played "Skip To My Lou And Others, Too." *Courtesy of Jean H. Karbler*

Congresswoman Marcy Kaptur, with an eagle saved by Back to the Wild, at the grand opening of Erie MetroParks' Community Foundation Preserve at Eagle Point, April 20, 2004. *Courtesy of Erie MetroParks*

School children on the new playground equipment donated by the Sandusky Rotary Club at Erie MetroParks' Osborn Park, July 26, 2004.

Courtesy of Erie MetroParks

Group who received the Hero and Red Cross Lifesaving Awards, October 2006, for saving the life of Sandra Schaefer after she suffered a cardiac arrest while working at NASA Plum Brook. Left to right: Stan Roberts, Halle Queen, Bill and Sandra Schaefer, Jim Pfleiger and Gary Ponikvar.

Courtesy of Brenda Bahnsen

Freshman baseball team at Perkins High School, 2004.

Courtesy of Lynne Thompson Daugherty

Mills Creek flooded onto the golf course, June 2006. *Courtesy of Cherie James*

Fifth-grade Perkins basketball team, 2006. Front row, left to right: Erin Sullivan, Chelsea Smith, Emily Oliver, Alexis Dixon, Kelsey Vaughn, Lauren Sheperd, Sydney Chicotel, Kimee Lipstraw and Maddie Mullins. In the second row are Amanda Wolf and Keli Daugherty. Third row: Coach Matso, Kendall Harris, Shannon Matso, Maryssa Engstrom, Shannon Ebert, Brianna Whitcombe and Darcy Daniel. In back is Coach Daniel.

Courtesy of Lynne Thompson Daugherty

Perkins Middle School basketball team, 2005–06. Front row, left to right: Nick Orshoski, Matt Stieroff, Miles Stieroff, Jordan Burrows and Andrew Zimmerman. Second row: Chris Baxter, Daniel Daugherty, Spencer Bryant, Nathan Mawhirter, Tom Barnum and Jarod Mariani. Back row: Coach Miller, Matt Hoty, Kyle Woodburn, Adam Ferback, Kevin Lipstraw and coach Shane Burrows. *Courtesy of Lynne Thompson Daugherty*

Sandusky State Theatre Stately Seats bench auction, 2004. Left to right: Peggy Scherer, Donald Schlett and Pat Ahner. All three were in the Sandusky High School class of 1941.

Courtesy of Linda Scherer

Prom-goers in Washington Park, 2005. Left to right: Paul Capizzi, Rachael Canterbury, Rich Niehm, Lena Camella, Christian McGory, Marley Gilchris, Lily Everson, Brandon Slater, David Ruff, Kaitlyn Nemeth, Brittany Rodisel, Spencer Farrar, Kate Barman, Travis Steinemann, Brooke Gilbert, Corey Nesbit, Corey Gilbert, Jaci Freitas, Nathan Singler and Chelsea Glorioso.
Courtesy of Barbara Ott

Sawmill Creek Golf and Mulligan's Pub staff, April 9, 2007. Left to right: Jerry Ehrhardt, Lorine Herb, Ken Neer, Doug Grubola, Shayne Fischer, Denise Schoen, Brenda Anderson, Evan Sager, Dave Johndon, Chris Bleile, Annie Bleile, Cindy Vajda, Bill Kenney, Kris Fischer, Mary Ann Jeffery and Craig Vajda. *Courtesy of Doug Grubola*

Ribbon-cutting ceremony at the grand opening of Erie MetroParks and the City of Sandusky's East Sandusky Bay Water Trail, June 2, 2007.
Courtesy of Erie MetroParks

Men's Garden Club of Erie County fundraising project, 2007. They are planting at Osborn Park, Huron Township. The money was used for scholarships for local students. *Courtesy of Floren V. James*

Following the Ohio Bike Week parade on Columbus Avenue, June 9, 2007. *Courtesy of Cherie James*

Family gathered for Sandusky native Daniel Albert's graduation from Ohio Wesleyan, May 2007. Front row, left to right: grandmother Helen Steinert, grandmother Jeanette Albert, Daniel, Rachel Ryan and Carol Albert. Back row: Donna Kastor, Mike Kastor, Ron Albert and David Albert. *Courtesy of Jeanette A. Albert*

Sandusky sisters graduating with a pharmacy degree from Ohio Northern University in Ada, Ohio, 2007. From left to right: Michael D. Kastor, Jenna Kastor, Kara Kastor and Donna J. Kastor. *Courtesy of Jeanette A. Albert*

Goodtime I docked at Kelleys Island, 2007. The group on the boat is having a bachelor and bachelorette party for Al Papenfuss and Dawn James who were getting married July 7, 2007. *Courtesy of Cherie James*

Forty-fifth reunion of Berlin Heights High School class of 1963, June 2008. Front row, left to right: Ron Johnson, Dick Koegle, Martha Palkovic Hoffman, Frances Church Houghtlen, Carol Churchill Genaway, Larry Cobb and Vicky Simonot Wagner. Back row: Melba Coughlin Hill, Valerie Dixon Pasqualini, Janet Skiver Schmidt, Rich Flecher, Carolyn Ward Blystone, Roger Massey, Susan Smith, Terry Plue and Marie Holzhauser Lowe. *Courtesy of Dick Koegle*

The CoCoBeanos at TGIFriday's on Cleveland Road, August 2007. Left to right: Scott Gast, Bryan Gast, Josh Post and Brian Runkle on drums. *Courtesy of George Gast*

Eric and Baylee Ward on a ride at Cedar Point, June 2007. *Courtesy of Kendra Ward*

Conrad and Elizabeth Gundlach family reunion at Osborn Park on Perkins Avenue in Huron, Aug. 3, 2008. *Courtesy of Tom and MaryLou Gundlach*

Russell family reunion, 2008. In front, left to right: Judy Baird, Mary Alice Hartenfield, Connie Russell, Jim Russell, Jeanette Albert and Diane Harbrecht. In back are Mike Kastor and Donna Kastor.
Courtesy of Jeanette A. Albert

Perkins sixth-grade Academic Challenge team at Adams Junior High, March 2008. Left to right: David Ahner, Thane Walton, Cody Dominick, Morgan Aaron, Maddie Hoelzer, Jacob Smith, Dave McDowell, Zach Weatherly, Hannah Wood and Alex Mack. *Courtesy of Sherri Dominick*

St. Mary's High School 58th class reunion at Osborn Park, August 2008. Front row, left to right: Mary Louise Seitz and Shirley Kreimes. Second row: Nancy Shepherd, Joyce Windau, John Viviano, Donna Guerra and Paulette Grahl. Back row: Ray Demres, Ann Hammond, Jim Westerhold, Jim Grathwol, Rich Grundler, Larry Schell, Edmond Andres, John Daniel, Rosemary Riccardi and Gerri Ruthsatz. *Courtesy of Sherri Dominick*

Rain during Ohio Bike Week on Columbus Avenue in downtown Sandusky, June 13, 2008. *Courtesy of Cherie James*

The John McCain for President bus arrives in Sandusky for a campaign visit from the presidential candidate, Oct. 30, 2008. *Courtesy of Ron Davidson*

Sen. John McCain addresses the crowd during a campaign stop in Washington Park, Oct. 30, 2008. *Courtesy of Sandusky Register*

Sandusky Choral Society at the 72nd Holiday Concert at Grace Episcopal Church, 2008. The director is William K. Kraus; James E. Gardner is the organist. *Courtesy of Jeanette A. Albert*

The "Cosmo" girls, May 2009. The women are all retired beauticians of Sandusky. From left to right: Alice Didion, Annette Churchill, Jan Ross, Roseann Kurilic, Lucy Stocker, Carol Kromer, Jeanette Albert and Delores Mentullo. Others in the group who were not present that day: Florence Byers, Orma Call, Marge Sidot, Barb Chambers, Bev Whetsol, Polly Smith and Sandy Mischler. *Courtesy of Jeanette A. Albert*

Perkins Middle School seventh-grade basketball champions, February 2009. Front row, left to right: Maxx Tamburrino, Connor Trent, Troy Aaron Jr., Dale Irby, Connor Mapus, Brock Broughton and Tanner Trent. Back row: assistant coach Len Broughton, Chase Green, David Doster, Nick Williams, Luke Fraley, Kyle Lewis, Alex Wilken, ballboy Matthew Schweinfurth, Cody Dominick and coach Matt Schweinfurth. *Courtesy of Sherri Dominick*

Bryan Gast of the band CoCoBeanos performs at Party at the Plaza, Mylander Plaza, July 24, 2009. *Courtesy of George Gast*